Search & Seizure Survival Guide

A FIELD GUIDE FOR LAW ENFORCEMENT

Anthony Bandiero

Blue to Gold Publishing

SPOKANE, WASHINGTON

Anthony Bandiero/Blue to Gold Publishing
www.BlueToGold.com
info@BlueToGold.com

Ordering Information:
Discounts are available on quantity purchases by government agencies, associations, and others. For details, contact "Bulk Sales" at the email address above.

Search & Seizure Survival Guide/Anthony Bandiero. —3rd ed.
ISBN 978-1981950256

Contents

Dedicated to Kristen, Carson, and Brandon

"We have an incredible warrior class in this country - people in law enforcement..., and I thank God every night we have them standing fast to protect us from the tremendous amount of evil that exists in the world."

—Brad Thor

How to use this Book

Your job as an officer is almost completely controlled by the Fourth Amendment. Think about it. Use of force, consensual encounters, arrests, vehicle searches, inventories, investigative detentions, patdowns, crime scenes, and on and on. All of these activities have one thing in common, they're all controlled by the Fourth Amendment.

There are only 54 words in the Fourth Amendment, yet authors have written millions of words trying describe just what those few words mean. As a law enforcement officer, you need a reference that can break down these important Constitutional doctrines into easy-to-apply-checklists. That's what this book does. If you need guidance in the field, pick-up this book. And when you get back to the station and need help articulating the legal standards for your report, pick-up this book.

There are other legal references out there and I highly recommend you read them. This book is not the end-all-be-all. But this book does have one serious competitive advantage: It was written by a former police officer who's been in your shoes and knows what you need to know.

If you have any suggestions, or need pointed in the right direction for a search and seizure dilemma you're facing, email me at info@bluetogold.com. Be safe.

The Amendments

First Amendment

Out of all of the rights discussed in this book, the First Amendment is one of the most protected. There are very few situations where you can regulate what someone says. Additionally, symbolic speech is protected and includes a person's right to burn an American flag in protest.[1]

Be very reluctant before you take any enforcement action against suspects who challenge you, yell at you, curse at you, or even challenge you to fight. My advice is to ignore it unless it's a legitimate safety issue (like telling a mob to attack you).

First Amendment

The following is a break down, part by part, of the First Amendment:

1. Congress shall make no law;

2. respecting an establishment of religion; or prohibiting the free exercise thereof;

3. or abridging the freedom of speech,

4. or of the press;

5. or the right of the people peaceably to assemble, and

6. to petition the government for a redress of grievances.

---

[1] Texas V. Johnson (U.S. Supreme Court, 1989)

Second Amendment

At the very core of the Second Amendment is the right of self-defense, especially while in your own home.[1] Still, governments can pass extensive regulations on firearms, like CCW requirements, barrel lengths, restricted carry inside bars, and so forth.[2]

Fortunately, these laws are pretty straightforward and are easy to enforce. Also, remember that whenever you detain a suspect you may disarm them, including those lawfully carrying a weapon. Your safety trumps their right to carry a weapon at that moment.

SECOND AMENDMENT

The following is a breakdown of the Second Amendment:

1. A well regulated militia, being necessary to the security of a free state; and

2. the right of the people to keep and bear arms, shall not be infringed.

---

[1] District Of Columbia V. Heller (U.S. Supreme Court, 2008)
[2] U.S. V. Miller (U.S. Supreme Court, 1939)

Fourth Amendment

Out of all of the Amendments, the Fourth Amendment is the most litigated. It is also the most important when it comes to your job as a police officer. At the core of every police action is the Fourth Amendment and you need to understand case law in order to do your job effectively and lawfully. That's what this book is all about.

FOURTH AMENDMENT

The Fourth Amendment is best understood as two separate parts.

Search and seizure clause:

1. The right of the people to be secure in their;

2. persons, houses, papers, and effects;

3. against unreasonable searches and seizures

4. shall not be violated; and

Search warrant clause:

1. no warrants shall issue, but upon probable cause;

2. supported by oath or affirmation;

3. and particularly describing the place to be searched;

4. and the persons or things to be seized.

Fifth Amendment

The Fifth Amendment is the most famous. Because of Hollywood everyone seems to *know* their rights. Yet the Fifth Amendment is extremely complex. For example, how many times has a suspect complained that you didn't read them their Miranda rights after an arrest, even though you didn't interrogate them? Better yet, what if you forget to read someone their rights and they confess? How do you fix that mistake? This book will give you the answers.

FIFTH AMENDMENT

There are a lot of subsections to the Fifth Amendment, and you probably won't deal with any of them except #4, the right against self-incrimination:

1. No person shall be held to answer for a capital, or otherwise infamous crime;

2. unless on a presentment or indictment of a grand jury, except in cases arising in the land or naval forces, or in the militia, when in actual service in time of war or public danger;

3. nor shall any person be subject for the same offense to be twice put in jeopardy of life or limb;

4. nor shall be *compelled* in any criminal case to be a witness against himself;

5. nor be deprived of life, liberty, or property, without due process of law;

6. nor shall private property be taken for public use, without just compensation.

The Right 'To be Left Alone'

The Supreme Court has recognized another right, though it is not solely defined in any particular amendment, and that is the right "to be left alone." (Note, the original phrase is the right "to be let alone." But I prefer "left alone.")

Whatever its source, whether common law, civil tort law, or the Bill of Rights, professional law enforcement officers must realize, and accept, that citizens have the right to be left alone. This is especially true today because more and more citizens are refusing police consensual encounters. I witnessed this first hand when subjects, who I wanted to talk with in order to develop intel, would bluntly ask me if they were free to go. When I replied yes, they would immediately leave (usually on their bicycle or moped). As Justice Brandies wrote in a dissenting opinion that was later endorsed by courts around the country;

> The makers of our Constitution undertook to secure conditions favorable to the pursuit of happiness. They recognized the significance of man's spiritual nature, of his feelings and of his intellect. They knew that only a part of the pain, pleasure and satisfactions of life are to be found in material things. They sought to protect Americans in their beliefs, their thoughts, their emotions and their sensations. They conferred, as against the Government, the right to be let alone—the most comprehensive of rights and the right most valued by civilized men. To protect that right, every unjustifiable intrusion by the Government upon the privacy of the individual, whatever the means employed, must be deemed a violation of the Fourth Amendment.[1]

---

[1] Olmstead v. United States, 277 U.S. 438 (U.S. 1928)

The Basics

Who is Protected

The Fourth Amendment protects everyone in the United States. The Fourth Amendment "is general and forbids every search that is unreasonable; it protects all, those suspected or known to be offenders as well as the innocent."[1] "A criminal may assert a violation of the Fourth Amendment just as well as a saint."[2] This is because the Fourth Amendment was forged to protect people from government abuse.[3]

The Fourth Amendment doesn't just apply to law enforcement officers. It applies to every government employee or agent that is enforcing a law, regulation or searching for evidence of wrongdoing. This includes health and building inspectors, safety inspectors, tax law enforcers, firemen and marshals, public school officials, government employee drug testers, and private individuals working on behalf of law enforcement.

CASE EXAMPLES

Foreign searches

DEA agents, working with Mexican authorities, conducted a warrantless search of a Mexican national's residence. The suspect was being held in the United States on drug charges. Since the search took place in a foreign country against a non-citizen, the Fourth Amendment was not applicable.[4]

Warrantless building inspections

An ordinance gave inspectors the right to enter any building in furtherance of code enforcement duties. An occupant demanded a warrant. The Court found the warrantless entries unlawful.[5]

---

[1] Go-Bart Importing Co. v. United States, 282 U.S. 344 (U.S. 1931)
[2] United States v. Washington, 573 F.3d 279 (6th Cir. Ohio 2009)
[3] 1-2 Search and Seizure § 2.10 (2015)
[4] United States v. Verdugo-Urquidez, 494 U.S. 259 (U.S. 1990)
[5] Camara v. Municipal Court of San Francisco, 387 U.S. 523 (U.S. 1967)

Private Searches

The Fourth Amendment controls government officials, not private citizens. There's no restriction on using information gained from a private citizen's search as long as they were not acting as a government agent.

An agent is anyone who conducts the search or seizure on your behalf. Government agents must abide by the same rules you do, otherwise agents become a loophole for violating the Fourth Amendment. As long as the citizen is not your agent, you can use any evidence they bring to you. But remember, you cannot exceed the original search conducted by the citizen unless you have exigency (rare) or a warrant.

REPORT WRITING

Articulate the following:

1. You didn't know or acquiesce in the private search and/or seizure; and

2. You didn't give permission to perform the search and/or seizure. Therefore, the citizen was furthering their own ends.

SAMPLE LANGUAGE

The key is to articulate that the private citizen was furthering his own ends when he conducted the search.

"I did not know or acquiesce in the private search conducted by Doe. Since I did not give permission to Doe he was furthering his own ends."

Reasonable Person

The ultimate touchstone of the Fourth Amendment is reasonableness.[1] In particular, the Fourth prohibits "unreasonable searches and seizures." In other words, if a search or seizure is *reasonable*, it's probably legal.

Yet, how do we define what's reasonable? Most of our definitions come from case law. What we can, and cannot, do is usually spelled out. But remember, courts don't' expect you to do your job perfectly, cops are humans and make mistakes. But you must be able to articulate *why* you're doing something. If you cannot it's probably unreasonable.

GUIDELINES

The "reasonable person" test asks, "not . . . what the defendant himself . . . thought, but what a *reasonable* man, *innocent* of any crime, would have thought had he been in the defendant's shoes."[2]

"An otherwise lawful seizure can violate the Fourth Amendment if it is executed in an unreasonable manner."[3]

Finally, the "Fourth Amendment does not mandate that police officers act flawlessly, but only that they act reasonably."[4]

---

[1] Riley v. California, 134 S. Ct. 2473 (U.S. 2014)
[2] United States V. Goddard (11th Circuit, 2002)
[3] United States V. Jacobsen (U.S. Supreme Court, 1992)
[4] United States V. Rohrig (6th Circuit, 1996)

Probable Cause

Articulating precisely the definition of "probable cause" is not possible. P/C is a fluid concept and whether or not you had P/C to arrest or conduct a search will be evaluated on a case-by-case basis. "On many occasions, we have reiterated that the probable-cause standard is a 'practical, nontechnical conception' that deals with the factual and practical considerations of everyday life on which reasonable and prudent men, not legal technicians, act."[1]

Probable cause to arrest

Probable cause to arrest exists, as the Court stated "where 'the facts and circumstances within [the arresting officer's] knowledge and of which they had reasonably trustworthy information [are] sufficient in themselves to warrant a man of reasonable caution in the belief that' an offense has been or is being committed,"[2] and that the defendant is the perpetrator.[3]

Probable cause to search

Probable cause to search, on the other hand, arises when there are reasonable grounds to believe, "not that the owner of the property is suspected of a crime, but that there is reasonable cause to believe that the specific 'things' to be searched for and seized are located on the property to which entry is sought,"[4] and there is probable cause to believe the things sought are evidence of a crime.[5] In fact, the identity of the offender need not be known.[6]

Cannot use discovered evidence as proof of probable cause

Finally, evidence found after a search cannot be used retroactively to establish probable cause.[7] It may be tempting to try to cure an

---

[1] Illinois v. Gates, 462 U.S. 213 (U.S. 1983)
[2] Draper v. United States, 358 U.S. 307 (U.S. 1959)
[3] United States v. Watson, 423 U.S. 411 (U.S. 1976)
[4] Zurcher v. Stanford Daily, 436 U.S. 547 (U.S. 1978)
[5] State v. Tamer, 475 So. 2d 918 (Fla. Dist. Ct. App. 3d Dist. 1985)
[6] State v. Warren, 301 S.E.2d 126 (N.C. Ct. App. 1983)
[7] Maryland v. Garrison, 480 U.S. 79 (U.S. 1987)

unlawful search by telling the prosecutor, "But I found 100 pounds of cocaine! There must have been probable cause." Similarly, just because the evidence sought was not found does not mean that there was no probable cause at the beginning.[1]

REPORT WRITING

P/C to arrest: Probable cause to arrest exists when the known facts and circumstances are sufficient to warrant a prudent person in believing that the suspect had *committed or was committing* an offense.

P/C to search: Probable cause to search exists where the known facts and circumstances are sufficient to warrant a man of reasonable prudence in the belief that contraband or evidence of a crime *will be* found in the place to be searched.

CASE EXAMPLES

Officer had probable cause to search vehicle

"There was probable cause to search a vehicle where police knew that a "blue compact station wagon" with four men in it had been circling a service station shortly before it was robbed by two men and sped away from an area near the scene shortly thereafter, that one occupant wore a green sweater as did one of the robbers, [and] that there was a trench coat in the auto similar to that worn by another of the robbers."[2]

Officer had probable cause that tied-off balloon contained narcotics

Where an officer observed a tied-off, uninflated opaque party balloon in a vehicle together with additional balloons, small plastic vials, and white powder in the glove compartment, and when the officer knew from his experience that such balloons were often used to deal drugs, probable cause existed to believe that the first balloon contained narcotics.[3]

---

[1] United States v. Gaschler, 2009 U.S. Dist. LEXIS 48449 (N.D. W. Va. June 3, 2009)
[2] Chambers v. Maroney, 90 S. Ct. 1975 (U.S. 1970)
[3] Tex. v. Brown, 103 S. Ct. 1535 (U.S. 1983)

Mistake of Law & Fact

The Supreme Court has long held that an officer's mistake of fact, as long as reasonable, will not invalidate reasonable suspicion or probable cause. And this makes sense. For example, if an officer observed two subjects in a fight, why should the officer be scrutinized if it turns out that they were merely play-fighting? Allowing mistake of fact recognizes that officers are human, work in an unpredictable environment, and should not wait until every fact or circumstance is verified before taking action. As the Supreme Court noted in 1949;

> But the mistakes must be those of reasonable men, acting on facts leading sensibly to their conclusions of probability. The rule of probable cause is a practical, nontechnical conception affording the best compromise that has been found for accommodating these often opposing interests. Requiring more would unduly hamper law enforcement. To allow less would be to leave law-abiding citizens at the mercy of the officers' whim or caprice.[1]

Mistake of law is a much higher standard and generally officers are not permitted to misunderstand the law. The Supreme Court said "an officer can gain no Fourth Amendment advantage through a sloppy study of the laws he is duty-bound to enforce."[2] For example, officers detained a suspect for drinking in public while in an apartment courtyard. A subsequent consent to search revealed drugs. The court held that the officers unreasonably misunderstood the law, as the courtyard was not a "public place."[3]

On the other hand, where officers enforced an ordinance that was later found to be unconstitutional the Court held that officers made a reasonable mistake of law, and evidence was not suppressed.[4]

---

[1] Brinegar v. United States, 338 U.S. 160 (U.S. 1949)
[2] Heien v. North Carolina, 135 S. Ct. 530 (U.S. 2014)
[3] People v. Krohn, 149 Cal. App. 4th 1294 (Cal. App. 4th Dist. 2007)
[4] Michigan v. DeFillippo, 443 U.S. 31 (U.S. 1979)

C.R.E.W.

The Supreme Court stated that all Fourth Amendment searches are presumed unreasonable unless there is a warrant or recognized exception. There are several exceptions, including "consent." C.R.E.W. is an acronym to help you remember this important limitation.

The "C" stands for consent. "R.E." stands for recognized exceptions. "W" stands for, yep you guessed it, warrant.

GUIDELINES

Whenever you conduct a search or seizure you need one of the following:

1. Consent

2. Recognized Exceptions

    - Exigency

    - Community caretaking

    - Reasonable suspicion

    - Probable cause arrest in public place

    - Mobile conveyance exception

    - Plain view (or smell, feel, hear)

    - Emergency searches

    - Hot/fresh pursuit

3. Warrant

What is a Search?

It is important to understand that the term "search," as used in this book at least, refers to conduct that invokes the protections of the Fourth Amendment. Police may engage in hundreds of "searches" every day, and yet invoke the Fourth Amendment only a few times.

For example, when police look into a stopped vehicle, they may be *searching* for weapons or contraband, but that conduct is not protected by the Fourth Amendment. In other words, just using your senses while lawfully positioned somewhere is not a Fourth Amendment search. On the other hand, opening the trunk of that same vehicle and looking around for contraband would be a protected search because that area is private.

There are two constitutional searches, a "physical intrusion" search or a search where a person has a reasonable expectation of privacy.

GUIDELINES

Physical intrusion:

1. An officer first makes a <u>physical trespass</u> and invades a "constitutionally protected area" enumerated in the Fourth Amendment ("persons, houses, papers, and effects"), and

2. The officer did it "for the purpose of obtaining information," or in "an attempt to find something."[1]

Reasonable expectation of privacy:

1. An individual must have exhibited an actual (subjective) expectation of privacy; and

2. That expectation must be one that society is prepared to recognize as reasonable (objective).[2]

---

[1] United States v. Jones, 132 S. Ct. 945 (U.S. 2012)
[2] Katz v. United States, 389 U.S. 347 (U.S. 1967)

Seizure of a Person

A seizure of the person is "taking possession" of a person such that he or she is not free to leave. Stated another way, a seizure occurs whenever a law enforcement officer meaningfully restricts a citizen's freedom of movement, for even a brief period of time.

> The test is necessarily imprecise because it is designed to assess the coercive effect of police conduct, taken as a whole, rather than to focus on particular details of that conduct in isolation. Moreover, what constitutes a restraint on liberty prompting a person to conclude that he is not free to "leave" will vary, not only with the particular police conduct at issue, but also with the setting in which the conduct occurs....[1]

There are two ways a person can be seized under the Fourth Amendment:

Physical seizure: This type of seizure occurs when you *intentionally* use *physical* force on a subject to restrict their movement.[2] It's important to remember that you must *intend* to seize someone under this standard. The suspect is seized once you intentionally *touch* them.[3]

Show of authority seizure: This type of seizure occurs when a person submits to your authority. This can occur by telling a suspect they are under arrest, or by pointing your gun. It can also occur when police show too much force for the situation, like during a consensual encounter. If a person disregards your authority and runs, they are not seized until they either give up or you restrain them.[4] Here, your intentions don't matter! What matters is what an objectively reasonable person would have thought from the defendant's point of view.

---

[1] Mich. v. Chesternut, 486 U.S. 567 (U.S. 1988)
[2] Brower v. County of Inyo, 489 U.S. 593 (U.S. 1989)
[3] United States V. Mcclendon (9th Circuit, 2013)
[4] California V. Hodari (U.S. Supreme Court, 1991)

REPORT WRITING

1. Before you can seize a person, you must have either reasonable suspicion ("R/S") or probable cause ("P/C");

2. If you only have R/S, you can use a minimal amount of force to affect the detention (be careful, too much force can be deemed excessive and/or de facto arrest requiring P/C);

3. If you have P/C, you can use reasonable force, except deadly force, to make the arrest. If the P/C is for a violent felony and the person would pose an imminent risk of substantial bodily harm or death to the public if allowed to escape, you can use deadly force to make the arrest and prevent escape.

CASE EXAMPLES

No seizure by DEA agents at airport

The defendant was not seized under the Fourth Amendment when she was asked by airport DEA agents if she would accompany them back to their office to discuss some discrepancies with her plane ticket. Once there, they asked for consent to search and she was informed of her right to refuse. She agreed and a female officer asked her to partially disrobe, after which bundles of heroin were discovered. The whole encounter was consensual.[1]

Consensual contacts on bus

Narcotics agents boarded a Greyhound bus and without any reasonable suspicion asked various passengers for consent to search their luggage. Arrested smuggler later argued that he was not free to leave, and therefore consent was tainted, because he was stuck on the bus in order to complete his journey. The Supreme Court disagreed, and stated that the test for a consensual encounter is not only the ability to leave, but also the ability to terminate the encounter. Defendant could have told the agents no without leaving the bus.[2]

---

[1] United States v. Mendenhall, 446 U.S. 544 (U.S. 1980)
[2] Fla. v. Bostick, 501 U.S. 429 (U.S. 1991)

Seizure of Property

A Fourth Amendment seizure occurs whenever you intentionally interfere with an individual's possessory interest in their property. The most important element here is intent. For example, if you blow a red light and run into another person's car, you have unintentionally interfered with their property and will be subject to tort liability, not a constitutional violation.

Remember you can be held vicariously liable if you "keep the peace" while someone takes another person's property. For example, if you're called to a civil standby while a subject removes property from a residence, it would be unwise to allow any disputed property to leave the residence.

GUIDELINES

A Fourth Amendment seizure of property occurs when you intentionally interfere with someone's possessory interest in their property.

CASE EXAMPLES

Officers that "kept the peace" liable for unlawful seizure of property
> Police were called to "keep the peace" while a trailer park manager illegally removed a mobile home for non-payment. The trailer was removed and the homeowner was told by police to not interfere with the park manager. The Supreme Court found that the police transformed the situation into an unlawful government seizure. [1]

---

[1] Soldal v. Cook County, 506 U.S. 56 (U.S. 1992)

Plain View

Under the plain view doctrine,[1] you can seize any item that is immediately apparent as contraband or evidence if you have legal access. This doctrine includes plain feel, plain smell,[2] and even "plain hearing."[3]

> "The rationale of the plain view doctrine is that if contraband is left in open view and is observed by a police officer from a lawful vantage point, there has been no invasion of a legitimate expectation of privacy and thus no search within the meaning of the Fourth Amendment—or at least no search independent of the initial intrusion that gave the officers their vantage point."[4]

REPORT CHECKLIST

Articulate the following:

1. You were lawfully present at the time of the observation. Under plain feel, the patdown for weapons must be lawful;

2. The item was immediately apparent as contraband or evidence;

3. You had lawful access to the item when you seized it.

SAMPLE LANGUAGE

The key is to articulate that the item was immediately apparent as evidence or contraband.

---

[1] Horton v. California, 496 U.S. 128 (U.S. 1990)
[2] Johnson v. United States, 333 U.S. 10 (U.S. 1948)
[3] People v. Bock Leung Chew, 142 Cal. App. 2d 400 (Cal. App. 1st Dist. 1956)
[4] Minn. v. Dickerson, 508 U.S. 366 (U.S. 1993)

"While conducting a patdown for weapons I felt an item in Doe's right front pants pocket that I immediately recognized to be a pipe for smoking narcotics... (explain why)."

"While walking up to the vehicle I heard the driver tell the passenger, "Quick, hide the gun, he's walking up." I made a warrantless search of the vehicle for the weapon. The driver was later determined to be a convicted felon."

CASE EXAMPLES

Plain view seizure during execution of arrest warrant is lawful

"One situation falling within the plain view doctrine involves the seizure of contraband while searching the home of a suspect subject to a valid arrest warrant. ... In this case, the law enforcement officers go into the residence based on a reasonable belief that the suspect is there and an arrest warrant founded on probable cause. ... After entering, they begin to search for the suspect. This effort sometimes necessitates looking in places where the suspect might be hiding. ... In the process, they come across an obviously incriminating object—that is, an object they have probable cause to believe is either evidence of a crime or contraband. ... Since the arrest warrant places them in a lawful position to view the incriminating object—by authorizing their presence in the residence—and the search for the suspect in places where he might be hiding establishes their lawful right of access to it, they can seize it without a search warrant."[1]

Seeing butt of gun is plain view

"An officer at the scene of an automobile stop, who can see the butt of a handgun under the passenger seat while standing outside the vehicle, can confiscate the gun under the plain-view exception to warrant requirement."[2]

---

[1] United States v. Munoz, 150 F.3d 401 (5th Cir. Tex. 1998)
[2] United States v. Campbell, 549 F.3d 364 (6th Cir. Tenn. 2008)

Single Purpose Container Doctrine

The single purpose container doctrine is an extension of the plain view doctrine. Here, an officer that sees a container and knows instantly what's inside. For example, a gun case, or a balloon containing heroin, or kilos of packaged cocaine. If officers see these items in plain view, and have lawful access, they can seize it as evidence.

REPORT WRITING

Articulate the following:

1. How you were lawfully positioned when you saw the item;

2. Why the contents of the item were immediately apparent as contraband (don't skimp here);

3. And if you seized the item, how you had lawful access.

CASE EXAMPLES

Convicted felon had no privacy in container labeled "gun case"

Defendant had no reasonable expectation of privacy in contents of case located in his residence and labeled as "gun case," and thus, police officers' warrantless search of the case after officers' valid entry into residence did not violate the Fourth Amendment, where officers knew that defendant was convicted felon prohibited from possessing guns.[1]

---

[1] United States v. Meada, 408 F.3d 14 (1st Cir. Mass. 2005)

Abandoned, Lost or Stolen Property

A person has no reasonable expectation of privacy in abandoned, lost or stolen property. The courts have defined abandonment broadly for search and seizure purposes. Abandonment occurs whenever a person leaves an item where the general public (or police) would feel free to access it. It can also occur whenever a person disowns property.

When it comes to abandonment, traditional property rights don't matter (i.e. a person could legally own an item, but still "abandon" it).[1] If abandonment occurs after an illegal detention, the evidence would be tainted and inadmissible.[2]

Additionally, if the defendant stole the item, like a purse or vehicle, he would not have a reasonable expectation of privacy in that item (but may have privacy in their own containers).

REPORT WRITING

Articulate the Following:

1. Where you found the property and how that location was accessible to the general public;

2. Why you thought the item was abandoned:

    o   Item appeared to be discarded;

    o   Left in a public area with no apparent owner around;

    o   Suspect told you it wasn't their property

    o   Suspect never asked for return of the property

---

[1] Stoner v. California, 376 U.S. 483 (U.S. 1964)
[2] People v. Verin, 220 Cal. App. 3d 551 (Cal. App. 1st Dist. 1990)

- ○ Suspect ditched property after seeing police

- ○ Property was abandoned/lost at a crime scene

3. What you did with the property. In particular, describe that your search could have been conducted by any member of the public.

SAMPLE LANGUAGE

The key is to articulate that the suspect had no reasonable expectation of privacy in the abandoned item. Also, describe how the search you conducted could have been performed by any member of the public.

"After responding to the residential burglary call I observed a black iPhone in the backyard. I confirmed with the homeowner that it was not his. Based on the totality of the circumstances, I determined that the item was abandoned and that the unknown owner (possibly suspect) had no reasonable expectation of privacy in the iPhone. I searched the cell phone and discovered…"

CASE EXAMPLES

No privacy in stolen property

"The Fourth Amendment does not protect a defendant from a warrantless search of property that he stole, because regardless of whether he expects to maintain privacy in the contents of the stolen property, such an expectation is not one that 'society is prepared to accept as reasonable.'"[1]

Suspect's abandonment was not voluntary

"When a person voluntarily abandons property, he forfeits any expectation of privacy that he might otherwise have had in it. … Here, [Defendant] denied that he owned the black bag only after he had been seized and handcuffed by the officers. Given this scenario, [Defendant]'s actions can hardly be characterized as a voluntary act."[2] Note: handcuffs alone don't mean a suspect cannot abandon property, but the court here felt that the suspect abandoned the property because of the highly intrusive form of detention. Again, each case is different and the key is to write a solid report!

---

[1] United States v. Caymen, 404 F.3d 1196 (9th Cir. Alaska 2005)
[2] United States v. Gwinn, 191 F.3d 874 (8th Cir. Mo. 1999)

Consensual Encounters

Consensual Encounter

The most common police encounter is the consensual one. You don't need a specific reason to speak with people and consensual encounters are a great way to continue an investigation when you have neither reasonable suspicion nor probable cause. As the Supreme Court said, "Police officers act in full accord with the law when they ask citizens for consent."[1]

Start the consensual encounter by asking a question. "Can I talk to you?" *Not*, "Come talk to me." Also, your conduct during the encounter must be reasonable. Lengthy encounters full of accusatory questioning will likely be deemed an investigative detention, not a consensual encounter.

REPORT WRITING

Articulate the following:

1. Describe your interactions with the suspect. Courts will ask if an objectively reasonable person would have felt free to leave or otherwise terminate the encounter;[2]

2. Describe the words used, and how the subject responded;

3. Describe your tone of voice and non-verbal communication (handshakes, smiling, etc.);

4. Describe any other relevant conduct;

5. Courts will look at the totality of the circumstances.

6. Remember, a subject does not have to answer any questions, including those seeking his identity. It would not be a crime if after asking for the subject's name he responded, "Mickey Mouse," and

---

[1] United States v. Drayton, 536 U.S. 194 (U.S. 2002)
[2] Fla. v. Bostick, 501 U.S. 429 (U.S. 1991)

walked away. DO NOT detain them for "contempt of cop" behavior.

SAMPLE LANGUAGE

The key is to articulate that an objectively reasonable person would feel free to leave or terminate the encounter.

"I decided to make a consensual encounter with the subject (not "suspect"). I walked up to him and in a conversational tone politely asked him if I could speak with him. (Explain the situation). Based on the totality of the circumstances, I believe an objectively reasonable person in the subject's position would feel free to leave or terminate the encounter."

CASE EXAMPLES

Order to come over and talk

Suspect was observed walking in mall parking lot when stores were closed. Officer said, "Come over here, I want to talk to you." Court held officer gave command to suspect and therefore needed reasonable suspicion. Evidence suppressed.[1]

Suspect fit drug courier profile

A suspect who fit the so-called "drug courier profile" was approached at an airport by two detectives. Upon request, but without oral consent, the suspect produced for the detectives his airline ticket and his driver's license. The detectives, without returning the airline ticket and license, asked the suspect to accompany them to a small room approximately 40 feet away, and the suspect went with them. Without the suspect's consent, a detective retrieved the suspect's luggage from the airline and brought it to the room. When the suspect was asked if he would consent to a search of his suitcases, the suspect produced a key and unlocked one of the suitcases, in which drugs were found. Court found this was not a consensual encounter and suppressed the evidence.[2]

---

[1] People v. Roth, 219 Cal. App. 3d 211 (Cal. App. 4th Dist. 1990)
[2] Fla. v. Royer, 460 U.S. 491 (U.S. 1983)

Consensual Encounter Investigative Activities

Just because you're engaged in a consensual encounter doesn't mean you can't investigate. However, be careful about how you go about it. Be cool, low key, and relaxed. Make small talk and just present yourself as a curious cop versus someone looking to make an arrest (though that may be your goal).

During a consensual encounter, there are really three investigative activities you can engage in; questioning, asking for ID, and seeking consent to search.

GUIDELINES

Questioning: "(L)aw enforcement officers do not violate the Fourth Amendment by merely approaching an individual on the street or in another public place, by asking him if he is willing to answer some questions, (or) by putting questions to him if the person is willing to listen."[1]

Identification: Asking for ID and running a subject for wants doesn't automatically convert encounter into a detention.[2] Hint, return ID as soon as possible so subject still "feels free to leave."[3]

Consent to search: As long as a subject is not illegally detained, you can always seek consent to search. The consent must be voluntary and the search conducted must not exceed any limitations, expressed or implied, by the subject (e.g. "you can search my car, but not my suitcase").[4]

---

[1] Fla. v. Royer, 460 U.S. 491 (U.S. 1983)
[2] People v. Bouser, 26 Cal. App. 4th 1280 (Cal. App. 4th Dist. 1994)
[3] United States v. Chan-Jimenez, 125 F.3d 1324 (9th Cir. Ariz. 1997)
[4] Bumper v. North Carolina, 391 U.S. 543 (U.S. 1968)

Asking for Identification

If you make a consensual encounter, you can always request that the subject identify themselves. But remember, there is no requirement that they do so. Additionally, there is likely no crime if the subject lied about their identity during a consensual encounter (however, possession of a fraudulent ID would be a crime).

REPORT WRITING

Articulate that you <u>asked</u> or <u>requested</u> identification, not that you demanded it.

SAMPLE LANGUAGE

The key is to articulate that you <u>asked</u> for identification and <u>did not keep it for longer than necessary</u>.

"I asked the subject if I could see his identification. He handed me a California driver's license and I ran the information through dispatch. I then handed the license back to the subject and did not keep it longer than necessary."

CASE EXAMPLES

Detaining a subject for identification requires reasonable suspicion

"When the officers detained [suspect] for the purpose of requiring him to identify himself, they performed a seizure of his person subject to the requirements of the Fourth Amendment.[1]

---

[1] Brown v. Tex., 99 S. Ct. 2637 (U.S. 1979)

Removing Hands from Pockets

Generally, you can always *ask* a subject to remove their hands from their pockets without worrying about converting the encounter into a detention. Courts understand the importance of officer safety.[1] What if the subject refuses to comply? If you can articulate a legitimate officer safety issue, then ordering a suspect to show his hands *may* be deemed reasonable.

An order to show hands does implicate the Fourth Amendment, however, because the interference with a person's freedom is so minimal it may fall under the minimal intrusion doctrine.

What if the suspect still refuses to show his hands and tries to leave? Remember, this is still a consensual encounter and if you decided to detain the subject you would need reasonable suspicion. An order to show hands may be a minimal intrusion, a detention is not.

REPORT WRITING

Request to show hands: If you ask a subject to show his hands articulate that it was done for <u>officer safety purposes</u>.

Order to show hands: If you order a subject to show his hands, explain why you were concerned for your safety. Then articulate that the order <u>was a minimal intrusion of the subject's freedom</u>.[2]

Note: This issue normally arises when the subject removes his hands from his pockets and forgot to let go of the drugs he just purchased. The subject then later argues in court that the request/order to remove hands was an unlawful order and therefore was a detention, not consensual encounter. If you focus on officer safety the court should hold your conduct as reasonable.

---

[1] People v. Franklin, 192 Cal. App. 3d 935 (Cal. App. 5th Dist. 1987)
[2] United States v. Enslin, 327 F.3d 788 (9th Cir. Cal. 2003)

Consent to Search

Absent good reason, you should *routinely* seek consent to search a person or their property even if you have reasonable suspicion or probable cause. Why? Because this will add an extra layer of protection to your case. For example, let's imagine you have probable cause to search a vehicle for drugs but still receive consent to search, the prosecution essentially needs to prove that consent was *freely and voluntarily* given.[1] If that fails, the prosecutor can always fall back on your probable cause. Without consent your case depends entirely on articulating P/C. Why not have both? Plus, juries like to see officers asking for consent. Either way, do your prosecutor a solid and write a complete and articulate report.

REPORT WRITING

Articulate the following:

1. Describe the environment, and particularly the lack of coercive police influences;

2. Describe the suspect and why you believed consent was <u>freely and voluntarily</u> given;

3. Describe how you asked for consent, in particular the words and tone you used;

4. Articulate how you complied with any limitations of scope, expressed or implied, by the suspect;

5. Finally, describe how the suspect was allowed to stop or modify the terms of the search while it was conducted.

Note: You must still articulate any R/S or P/C you had in your report, otherwise the case may rest entirely on your consent to search.

---

[1] Bumper v. North Carolina, 391 U.S. 543 (U.S. 1968)

A suspect's refusal to consent to search may not be used to build reasonable suspicion or probable cause.[1] Your report should state that the suspect denied consent, but don't articulate his refusal created further suspicion.

Sample Language

The key is to articulate that the consent was freely and voluntarily given.

"I asked Doe for consent to search his vehicle for drugs and weapons. (Describe encounter and language used.) Based on the totality of the circumstances, I believe the consent to search provided by Doe was freely and voluntarily given."

Case Examples

"I don't care"

Suspect was stopped for speeding. He was suspected of drug possession and officer asked for consent to search. Suspect responded, "I don't care." Search revealed crack cocaine. Suspect's statement implied consent to search.[2]

Patdown of suspect who wanted to get out of vehicle upheld

Vehicle was stopped for an equipment violation. Driver wanted to get out and see proof that his taillight was broken. Officer said only on the condition that he be subject to a patdown. Suspect said "that was fine" and stepped out. Patdown revealed drugs. Suspect voluntarily submitted to patdown.[3] (What an idiot!)

No need to inform suspect they have a right to refuse search

Police stopped the car for an equipment violation. Officer asked driver if he could search the car. Driver responded, "Sure, go ahead." Officer found forged checks. Driver argued he was not informed of his right to refuse and therefore illegal search. Knowledge of the right to refuse is just one factor in judging voluntariness. Search upheld.[4]

---

[1] United States v. White, 890 F.2d 1413 (8th Cir. Mo. 1989)
[2] United States v. Polly, 630 F.3d 991 (10th Cir. Okla. 2011)
[3] State v. Cunningham, 26 N.E.3d 21 (Ind. 2015)
[4] Schneckloth v. Bustamonte, 412 U.S. 218 (U.S. 1973)

Consensual Transportation

There is no Fourth Amendment violation if you consensually transport a subject to the police station for a consensual interview or to a crime scene. The key is that the subject's consent must be freely and voluntarily given.

REPORT WRITING

If you consensually transport a subject to another location, like the police station, articulate that the suspect wanted to be transported.

SAMPLE LANGUAGE

The key is to articulate that the transportation was consensual.

"Doe agreed to be consensually interviewed at the police station but said he did not have transportation. I asked if he needed a ride and he said, "Yes." I offered to transport him to the station in my marked patrol unit. I asked Doe if he would mind if I patted him down for weapons for my safety, and he agreed to a patdown. I did not find any weapons and he was transported in the back of the patrol car to the station without restraints or other arrest-like treatment. Based on the totality of the circumstances I believe that the transportation was consensual."

CASE EXAMPLES

No violation when a person agrees to accompany police

Appellate courts have held that when a person agrees to accompany the police to a station for interrogation or some other purpose, the Fourth Amendment is not violated.[1]

---

[1] In re Gilbert R., 25 Cal. App. 4th 1121 (Cal. App. 2d Dist. 1994)

Knock and Talks

There is no Fourth Amendment violation if you try to consensually contact a person at their home.[1] The key to knock and talks is to comply with social norms. Think about it this way, if the Girl Scouts could do it, so could you.

You must be reasonable when you contact the subject. Incessant pounding on the door, for example, would likely turn the encounter into a detention if the subject knows that it's the police doing it (an objectively reasonable person would believe that police are commanding them to open the door). Likewise, waking a subject up at 3 a.m. was viewed as a detention requiring reasonable suspicion.[2] Again, if the Girl Scouts wouldn't do then it's probably unreasonable.

What about "No Trespass" signs? You can usually ignore them because trying to have a consensual conversation with someone is not what is typically meant by trespassing. Same goes with "no soliciting" signs.

REPORT WRITING

Articulate the following:

1. Where you made contact with the subject (i.e. front door). If contact was made other than the front door articulate why. This is very important because you may have violated a home's curtilage and therefore implicated the Fourth Amendment;

2. Describe how you made contact (knocked twice, doorbell, etc.);

3. Describe the conversation you had and how it was voluntary;

4. If the subject terminated the conversation articulate how you immediately left the residence.

---

[1] United States v. Crapser, 472 F.3d 1141 (9th Cir. Or. 2007)
[2] United States v. Jerez, 108 F.3d 684 (7th Cir. Wis. 1997)

Sample Language

The key is to articulate that the knock and talk complied with <u>social norms</u>.

"In an attempt to make a consensual encounter with John Doe I knocked on his apartment door on January 1, 2017 at 2 p.m. I did not command Doe to open the door. He opened the door within approximately 30 seconds. Based on the totality of the circumstances I believe the knock and talk complied with social norms."

Case Examples

Knock and talk at 4 a.m. held invalid

Officers went to suspect's residence at 4 a.m. with the sole purpose to arrest him. There was no on-going crime and the probable cause was based on an offense that occurred the previous night. Violation of knock and talk because officers exceeded social norms.[1]

Persistent knock in the middle of the night not consensual

Officers knocked on motel room door in middle of night for a full three minutes in order to make the occupant answer. Conduct constitutes investigative detention, not consent.[2]

Command to open door was not a consensual encounter

"Officers were stationed at both doors of the duplex and (an officer) had commanded (defendant) to open the door. A reasonable person in (defendant's) situation would have concluded that he had no choice but to acquiesce and open the door."[3]

Constant pressure to consent to search held unlawful

During knock and talk officers continued to press defendant for permission to enter and search. Later consent-to-search was product of illegal detention.[4]

---

[1] United States v. Lundin, 47 F. Supp. 3d 1003 (N.D. Cal. 2014)
[2] United States v. Jerez, 108 F.3d 684 (7th Cir. Wis. 1997)
[3] United States v. Poe, 462 F.3d 997 (8th Cir. Mo. 2006)
[4] United States v. Washington, 387 F.3d 1060 (9th Cir. Nev. 2004)

Providing False ID

If you make a consensual encounter the subject is not required to tell the truth. This includes lying about their identity. This issue causes many officers heartburn because many believe that once someone lies about their identity they have committed a crime. That is false.

Remember, consensual encounters are *voluntary*. Your conversation may prove worthwhile, or it may be a complete waste of time.

Note, if a person is detained or arrested, they cannot lie about their identity. Also, a few states and the feds make it illegal to lie about a material fact, even if during a consensual encounter. Check first.

GUIDELINES

A person is under no legal obligation to tell the truth when police make a consensual encounter. Do not take any enforcement action if a person lies, including lying about their identity.

CASE EXAMPLES

Providing false name not a crime unless lawfully detained or arrested

Defendant's arrest was premised on his having given a false name. The state statute criminalizes a person's false representation or identification of himself or herself to a peace officer "upon a lawful detention or arrest of [that] person ...." The law applies only where the false identification is given in connection with lawful detention or arrest, and does not apply to consensual encounters with police. Since defendant's subsequent arrest was based upon an unlawful detention, and the search incident to the arrest was likewise unlawful suppression is required of contraband seized after search incident to unlawful arrest.[1]

---

[1] People v. Walker, 210 Cal. App. 4th 165 (Cal. App. 6th Dist. 2012)

Investigative Detentions

Overview of Detentions

If you have articulable reasonable suspicion that a suspect is involved in criminal activity, you may briefly detain them in order to "maintain the status quo" and investigate.[1] Courts use the "status quo" language because it implies that you're not really doing anything to the suspect, besides taking some of their time. This distinction is important because all Fourth Amendment intrusions must be reasonable. If all you're doing is temporarily detaining a suspect, versus conducting a full search or other arrest-like behavior, then it's more likely to be considered reasonable.

REPORT WRITING

1. Try to seek consent first. If that fails, tell them they're being detained;

2. Fully articulate why you thought criminal activity was afoot (even if you had consent). Remember, reasonable suspicion must be individualized. If you thought a person was selling drugs, you're not allowed to automatically detain his friend, unless you articulate that he was also involved;

3. If you used any force, including handcuffs or pointing a firearm, you must articulate why, and how that force was the least intrusive under the circumstances;

4. Finally, you must diligently pursue the investigation in order to confirm or dispel your suspicions.[2] If your suspicions are reasonably dispelled, the suspect must be allowed to leave or otherwise terminate the encounter. If needed, convert the stop to a consensual encounter. "Thank you for your cooperation. *You're free to go* but before you do can I ask you a few more questions?"

---

[1] Terry v. Ohio, 392 U.S. 1 (U.S. 1968)
[2] United States v. Sharpe, 470 U.S. 675 (U.S. 1985)

Duration of Investigative Detentions

Whenever you detain someone for reasonable suspicion, you must diligently pursue a means of investigation that is likely to confirm or dispel the suspicion quickly.[1] Once your suspicion has been dispelled, the citizen must be allowed to go on their way. If you still have a "hunch" you want to pursue, convert the stop to a consensual encounter.

REPORT WRITING

1. Describe how you worked diligently to <u>confirm or dispel</u> your reasonable suspicion;

2. If any force was used, describe how that force was the <u>minimal necessary to maintain the status quo</u> and conduct your investigation. Maintaining status quo means that in order to conduct your investigative detention, you must effectively "freeze" the scene or suspect.

3. Overall, investigative detentions must be reasonable in time, place and manner.[2]

CASE EXAMPLES

Detention must be brief

"In Terry, we held that an officer may, consistent with the Fourth Amendment, conduct a brief, investigatory stop when the officer has a reasonable, articulable suspicion that criminal activity is afoot.[3]

---

[1] United States v. Sharpe, 470 U.S. 675 (U.S. 1985)
[2] Terry v. Ohio, 392 U.S. 1 (U.S. 1968)
[3] Illinois v. Wardlow, 120 S. Ct. 673 (U.S. 2000)

De Facto Arrests

If a court considers an investigative detention unreasonable, it will become a de facto arrest requiring probable cause. In particular, courts will scrutinize the use of firearms, handcuffs, involuntary transportation, and placing suspect in a locked patrol car. If you don't have probable cause you can get sued for violating constitutional rights or criminally charged for false imprisonment.

REPORT WRITING

Courts look at the following factors:

1. Purpose behind the stop and nature of the crime (the more serious the crime, the less likely your tactics will be unreasonable);

2. Whether the officer worked diligently to confirm or dispel the suspicion;

3. Amount of force used, and the need for such force;

4. Extent suspect's freedom was restrained;

5. Number of officers involved;

6. Duration and intensity of the stop;

7. Time and location of stop; and

8. The need for immediate action.

Handcuffs, Firearms, and Use of Force During R/S Stops

Generally, if you handcuff a suspect, point a firearm, or use force during an investigative detention, it will be deemed an arrest requiring probable cause.

There are exceptions, but you need to have legitimate reasons. If you make a reasonable suspicion stop on a suspect you believe is about to pull a gun on you, then of course you get point your firearm on them and conduct a patdown! Your safety comes first. But articulate it in your report. Similarly, if you believe a suspect is about to run, then handcuff him. Again, articulate this in your report.

REPORT WRITING

Handcuffing:
> You may handcuff a suspect if you can articulate they present a physical threat or are about to flee.[1]

Firearms:
> You may point your firearm at a suspect only if you can articulate that it's necessary given the seriousness of the situation.[2]

Use of Force:
> You're allowed to use a minimal amount of force to detain a non-compliant suspect. But again, articulate exactly why you did what you did.

---

[1] People v. Stier, 168 Cal. App. 4th 21 (Cal. App. 4th Dist. 2008)
[2] People v. Dolly, 128 Cal. App. 4th 1354 (Cal. App. 2d Dist. 2005)

Unprovoked Flight

If you are patrolling a "high crime" area and a person suddenly, and without provocation, runs upon seeing you, these may be sufficient conditions to conduct an investigative detention in order to determine whether they are involved in criminal activity.[1] Unprovoked flight, by itself, doesn't provide sufficient reason to conduct a patdown. You need to articulate something more such as a known gang member, history of violence, or possible drug *dealer* (not simply drug *user*).

Finally, this rule may also include wealthy areas where a rash of recent burglaries have occurred, or a business district when all the stores are closed. Articulate, articulate, articulate. Then articulate more.

REPORT WRITING

1. Describe why the area you were patrolling was a <u>high crime area</u>;

2. Describe exactly what the subject did <u>upon seeing the police</u>, if accurate, describe the run as a <u>headlong flight consummate with evasion</u>;

3. Articulate whether you were in a marked unit, or a common identifiable unmarked police vehicle (remember, must be flight upon seeing police). Describe how you <u>ordered the suspect to stop running from the police</u> (important before using physical force);

4. Finally, <u>articulate exactly what force you used</u> and how that was reasonable under the circumstances.

•   If the suspect discards contraband *before* you capture him, it can be admitted as evidence even if the court later finds that the initial reason for detention lacked reasonable suspicion.

---

[1] Illinois v. Wardlow, 528 U.S. 119 (U.S. 2000)

Patdowns

A patdown (or Terry frisk) is a limited search for weapons. You must articulate two things before you can conduct a patdown. First, the investigative stop itself must be lawful (based on individualized reasonable suspicion). Second, you must articulate that the person is armed and dangerous.

REPORT WRITING

Courts consider the following factors:

1. Past criminal history;

2. Bulge in clothing consistent with a weapon;

3. Furtive movements;

4. The suspect's words, clothing and actions;

5. Reliable tip that suspect was armed;

6. Whether the crime you're investigating is one commonly associated with weapons (burglary, robbery, violent domestic battery);

7. And other articulable reasons.

Reminder: If the stop involves a crime of violence, or crime involving any weapon, you can <u>automatically conduct a patdown</u>.

CASE EXAMPLES

Officer doesn't need to be certain

"The officer need not be absolutely certain that the individual is armed; the issue is whether a reasonably prudent man in the circumstances would be warranted in the belief that his safety or that of others was in danger."[1]

Relevant considerations

Relevant considerations may include: observing a visible bulge in a person's clothing that could indicate the presence of a weapon; seeing a weapon in an area the suspect controls, such as a car; 'sudden movements' suggesting a potential assault or 'attempts to reach for an object that was not immediately visible'; 'evasive and deceptive responses' to an officer's questions about what an individual was up to; unnatural hand postures that suggest an effort to conceal a firearm; and whether the officer observes anything during an encounter with the suspect that would dispel the officer's suspicions regarding the suspect's potential involvement in a crime or likelihood of being armed.[2]

Refusal to remove hands is a factor justifying frisk

"The officers, after initiating the stop, twice ordered that [defendant] remove his hands from his pockets, which he refused to do. The report of an assault in progress, the matching description, and the additional factors that supported the stop provided the officers with reason to believe that [defendant] was armed and dangerous, and that the refusal to remove his hands was an effort to conceal a weapon.[3]

Stop in gang-ridden area helped justify patdown

"[T]the area in which the incident occurred gave police officers particular reason to be concerned about the possibility of gun-related violence. The neighborhood was known as a high-crime area of the city; but more importantly, there were indications of gang activity, recent reports of shots fired, and the occurrence of a drive-by shooting with two victims two days earlier and one block away from the location where the men were discovered drinking. These specific and recent indicia of violence, including gun-related violence, increased the odds that an individual detained at this location for apparent criminal activity (even a petty offense like the one at issue here) might be armed."[4]

---

[1] Terry v. Ohio, 392 U.S. 1 (U.S. 1968)
[2] Thomas v. Dillard, 818 F.3d 864 (9th Cir. Cal. 2016)
[3] United States v. Simmons, 560 F.3d 98 (2d Cir. 2009)
[4] United States v. Patton, 705 F.3d 734 (7th Cir. Ill. 2013)

Patdowns Based on Anonymous Tips

A patdown (or Terry frisk) is a limited search for weapons. If police receive an anonymous tip that someone is illegally carrying a weapon, the tip must be proved reliable.[1] Typically, this means that the tip must predict future behavior and is corroborated by personal observations. The Supreme Court stated that a lower standard would likely apply to schools and airports.

REPORT WRITING

1. Articulate what information was provided by the anonymous person. For our purposes, an anonymous tipster is anyone who refuses to "get involved" or identify themselves;

2. Describe what information provided by the tipster was corroborated by future behavior.[2] Also describe any other information that could not have been known by just any member of the general public;

3. Articulate other safety concerns (near school, stadium, church, etc.);

4. If possible, try to get consent to search. Articulate the suspect's response and whether he refused consent;

5. Finally, document the search whether or not a weapon was found.

---

[1] Fla. v. J.L., 529 U.S. 266 (U.S. 2000)
[2] Ala. v. White, 496 U.S. 325 (U.S. 1990)

Detentions Based on Anonymous Tips

Police may make an investigative detention based on an anonymous tip if the information has some indicia of reliability and the information is independently corroborated.[1] The courts will use the totality of the circumstances test and it's vital you articulate all pertinent facts and circumstances in your report.

REPORT WRITING

1. Amount of detail provided (especially details that the general public would not know);

2. Describe what information was <u>corroborated by future behavior;</u>[2]

3. Whether the information was based on <u>first-hand observations</u>;

4. Whether the tip came through 911 or face-to-face;

5. Whether the source was involved in illegal conduct and they are putting their anonymity in jeopardy by providing information to police; and

6. The timeliness of the report (the more recent the better because the informant has less time to create a lie).

---

[1] Navarette v. California, 134 S. Ct. 1683 (U.S. 2014)
[2] Ala. v. White, 496 U.S. 325 (U.S. 1990)

Involuntary Transportation

In general, involuntarily transportation of a suspect back to the crime scene for identification[1] will be considered a formal arrest requiring probable cause.[2] But like all good rules there are exceptions.

REPORT WRITING

During some particularly serious investigations you may have no choice but to transport the suspect. Just like the use of firearms or handcuffs will not always covert an investigative detention into an arrest, transporting a suspect against his will doesn't always equal arrest.

Articulate the following:

- You asked for consent to transport suspect and were denied;

- You told the suspect that he wasn't under arrest;

- The nature of the offense was serious (rape, murder, robbery);

- Involuntary transport was the least intrusive means available to confirm or dispel your suspicions.

SAMPLE LANGUAGE

The key is to articulate <u>exigency</u>.

"While responding to the report of a sexual assault, I was informed of the suspect's description by on-scene officers. I found a suspect matching that description (describe why and where). I made an investigative detention on the suspect (describe response and additional evidence). I was told by Officer Jones that the victim was going to be transported to ABC hospital and there were obvious signs

---

[1] Hayes v. Florida, 470 U.S. 811 (U.S. 1985)
[2] Dunaway v. New York, 442 U.S. 200 (U.S. 1979)

of a violent sexual assault. I asked the suspect if he would voluntarily go back to the scene for further investigation and he said "No." Based on the totality of the circumstances, I believed exigency existed and I involuntarily transported Doe two blocks back to the scene where the victim positively identified Doe as the perpetrator." Obviously, a report like this would be very long, articulate everything.

CASE EXAMPLES

Transport away from "hostile crowd" upheld

A hostile crowd, in a high-crime area, gathered around detention stop. Officer's involuntary movement away from scene upheld.[1]

Valid transportation to find out what happened to children

A female walked into the police station and said that she had "done something very bad" to her children. An officer then told her she was not under arrest, but that he would drive her home to find out what happened. Officer discovered three of the six children were shot and killed. This was a lawful detention, not an arrest.[2]

Transport to ID suspect upheld in gang rape

An officer investigating a brutal gang rape stopped two suspects. They did not speak English and the officer handcuffed them and transported them to the hospital for identification. The involuntary transport was reasonable under the circumstances and evidence not suppressed.[3]

Involuntary transportation for questioning unlawful

Officers picked up suspect, took him downtown for questioning, and eventually obtained a confession. The officers contended that the suspect was just being "detained" for questioning, but the Supreme Court disagreed, ruling that the movement resulted in the arrest of the defendant. Confession suppressed.[4]

---

[1] People v. Courtney, 11 Cal. App. 3d 1185 (Cal. App. 1st Dist. 1970)
[2] United States v. Charley, 396 F.3d 1074 (9th Cir. Cal. 2005)
[3] In re Carlos M., 220 Cal. App. 3d 372 (Cal. App. 4th Dist. 1990)
[4] Dunaway v. New York, 442 U.S. 200 (U.S. 1979)

Detaining Victims & Witnesses

Generally, you cannot force a victim or witness to cooperate with your investigation. It is a "settled principle that while the police have the right to request citizens to answer voluntarily questions concerning unsolved crimes they have no right to compel them to answer."[1]

If you have located an uncooperative material witness, and they are *vital* for your investigation, then identify them. Give their information to the prosecutor and let her decide whether or not they should be subpoenaed.

GUIDELINES

Victims: Do not detain a hostile victim and order them to cooperate with your investigation.

Witnesses: Two situations where you can detain a witness:

1. The Supreme Court upheld a temporary roadblock to identify witnesses to a fatal hit and run one week after the accident;[2]

2. If a crime has just been committed, and you can articulate exigent circumstances, you can briefly detain a witness in order to record a statement or identify them for later contact.

---

[1] Davis v. Mississippi, 394 U.S. 721 (U.S. 1969)
[2] Illinois v. Lidster, 540 U.S. 419 (U.S. 2004)

Fingernail Scrapes

If you have reasonable suspicion or probable cause to believe a suspect committed a crime, and currently has evidence underneath their fingernails, you can conduct a warrantless "scrape" and retrieve any evidence such as dirt, blood, DNA and so forth. You're allowed to use the minimal force necessary to recover the evidence.

REPORT WRITING

1. Articulate what R/S or P/C you had against the suspect;

2. Describe why you thought the suspect had evidence underneath their fingernails (visible foreign material);

3. If you asked for consent (and you should), share whether it was granted or denied;

4. Either way, articulate that the warrantless search could have been conducted for two reasons; fingernail scrapes are a very limited intrusion and the ready destructibility of the evidence.

CASE EXAMPLES

Warrantless scrape of fingernails upheld

The defendant was questioned by the police regarding the murder of his wife. During the questioning, police noticed dark stains under his fingernails. The police asked if they could scrape under his nails. After refusing permission, police seized the defendant and scraped the debris, which proved to contain traces of the deceased's blood as well as fabric from her nightgown. The Court found that the nature of the evidence justified the immediate action of the police.[1]

---

[1] Cupp v. Murphy, 412 U.S. 291 (U.S. 1973)

Fingerprinting

If you have reasonable suspicion that a suspect committed a crime you can take their fingerprints in the field if you articulate that it would help solve the crime. For example, if you make an investigative detention on a burglary suspect, you could take their fingerprints in order to match them to any prints found on scene. You should not involuntarily transport the suspect so take prints in the field.

REPORT WRITING

1. Articulate what reasonable suspicion you had against the suspect;

2. Describe why you thought the suspect's fingerprints could assist in the investigation;

3. If you asked for consent (and you should), share whether it was granted or denied;

4. If consent is denied, articulate that the warrantless taking of fingerprints is an investigative technique that's minimally intrusive and will help confirm or deny your suspicions.

CASE EXAMPLES

Police can obtain fingerprints with reasonable suspicion

"There is support...that the Fourth Amendment would permit seizures for the purpose of fingerprinting, if there is a reasonable basis for believing that fingerprinting will establish or negate the suspect's connection with that crime."[1]

---

[1] Hayes v. Florida, 105 S. Ct. 1643 (U.S. 1985)

Public Recordings

Generally, you have no right to stop a person from recording your public activities.[1] Do not engage the person unless you have specific articulable reasonable suspicion they are engaged in criminal activity. This is rarely the case and 99% of the time these people want to catch you doing something stupid so it goes viral on YouTube.

Additionally, if you lawfully stop or detain a person who is recording you, and you have R/S that they are dangerous, you can order them to put their phone away for officer safety purposes. But don't order them to stop recording unless you can articulate legitimate officer safety reason or distraction (e.g. streaming to Facebook live).

GUIDELINES

A citizen may lawfully record your activities in public. If you order a suspect to put their phone away for officer safety purposes, do not also order them to turn off the recording, unless you have a legitimate reason.

Some recordings that constitute criminal activity include:

- Invasion of privacy;

- Recording NCIC information on your in-car computer;

- Recording a building in preparation of an active shooter or terrorist attack.

If the person is interfering with your investigation, like yelling or too close to the scene, give them orders to quiet down or move back. But be professional and explain what you want done and why. If you contemplate an arrest of a "Cop Block" type of person, get supervisor approval (and support) for the arrest if possible since there will likely be a complaint and maybe lawsuit.

---

[1] Glik v. Cunniffe, 655 F.3d 78 (1st Cir. Mass. 2011)

Arrests

Arrest Warrants

An officer may make a probable cause arrest in any place where the officer is legally present. Usually, this is in public places or in private places where officers are investigating a crime. If an officer intends to enter a suspect's home to make an arrest, an arrest warrant will typically be required. The arrest warrant can be a bench warrant, misdemeanor traffic warrant, or felony warrant.

GUIDELINES

An officer may enter a suspect's home if:

1. An arrest warrant has been issued for the suspect;

2. Police have probable cause to believe the suspect is presently in his home;

3. Police abide by knock and announce rules;

4. Upon entry, police may look in people-sized areas;

5. Once the arrest is complete, police cannot stay and search for evidence without an additional search warrant or consent.

CASE EXAMPLES

An arrest warrant authorizes entry into the suspect's home

"For Fourth Amendment purposes, an arrest warrant founded on probable cause implicitly carries with it the limited authority to enter a dwelling in which the suspect lives when there is reason to believe the suspect is within."[1]

---

[1] Payton v. New York, 445 U.S. 573 (U.S. 1980)

Lawful Warrantless Arrest

Officers make millions of warrantless arrests every year. Though there may be additional state laws in play (e.g. cannot arrest for misdemeanor not committed in your presence), the 4th Amendment is not violated as long as you have probable cause, authority to make the arrest, and lawful access to the suspect.

GUIDELINES

A constitutional arrest has three components:

1. Probable cause;

2. Legal authority to make the arrest; and

3. Lawful access to the suspect;[1]

CASE EXAMPLES

If arrest is based on any probable cause, arrest is constitutional

"The standard of probable cause applies to all arrests, without the need to 'balance' the interests and circumstances involved in particular situations. If an officer has probable cause to believe that an individual has committed even a very minor criminal offense in his presence, he may, without violating the Fourth Amendment, arrest the offender."[2] Note, still abide by your agency/state rules.

Warrantless arrest inside private office unlawful

It was illegal for police, without consent, exigent circumstances, or a warrant, to go past a receptionist and enter the locked office of an attorney to arrest him for selling cocaine.[3]

---

[1] Payton v. New York, 445 U.S. 573 (U.S. 1980)
[2] Atwater v. City of Lago Vista, 532 U.S. 318 (U.S. 2001)
[3] People v. Lee, 186 Cal. App. 3d 743 (Cal. App. 4th Dist. 1986)

Committed in Officer's Presence Requirement

If a law enforcement officer has probable cause to believe that an individual has committed even a very minor criminal offense in his or her presence, the officer may arrest the offender without violating the Fourth Amendment.[1]

Additionally, most jurisdictions hold that a warrantless misdemeanor arrest may only be made for an offense which the officer has probable cause to believe was committed "in the presence" of the arresting officer. Under this requirement, the officer must perceive the acts or events which constitute the offense while they are taking place, and not merely learn of them at a later time.

REPORT WRITING

Articulate the following:

1. Articulate what you saw, smelled, heard, or felt and what crime you believed was committed;

2. If the entire criminal act was not completed in your presence, articulate what elements of the crime occurred in your presence.

CASE EXAMPLES

Hearing assault is committed within officer's presence

As the officer was walking up to the residence he heard suspect say, "I'm going to kill you bitch" then heard and saw wife go back against a wall. He did not see suspect touch his wife. Court held battery was committed within the officer's presence.[2]

---

[1] Atwater v. City of Lago Vista, 532 U.S. 318 (U.S. 2001)
[2] State v. Forsythe, 194 W. Va. 496 (W. Va. 1995)

Arrestable Violations

When you arrest a person, there is no legal obligation to charge every violation for which you have probable cause ("P/C"). Even if the charged offense is later found to lack P/C, any violation for which you had valid P/C, if even not charged, will make the arrest constitutional.

REPORT WRITING

If you have probable cause that a suspect committed an offense, articulate it in your report, even if not charged. This will help protect you from lawsuits if the charged offense is later found to lack P/C. Any valid P/C will make the arrest constitutional.

CASE EXAMPLE

Any probable cause will make arrest lawful

If an officer has probable cause to believe that an individual has committed even a very minor criminal offense in his presence, he may, without violating the Fourth Amendment, arrest the offender.[1] In Atwater, an officer arrested an uncooperative mother for not wearing her seatbelt. The arrest violated state law, but the Supreme Court said that even if the officer used "poor judgment," it did not violate the Fourth Amendment. Best practice: Do not violate your agency policy or state law. Your supervisor and chief won't be happy no matter what your close friends on the Supreme Court say.

---

[1] Atwater v. City of Lago Vista, 532 U.S. 318 (U.S. 2001)

Stale Misdemeanor Rule

In some states, like California, an officer cannot unnecessarily delay making an arrest for a misdemeanor crime committed in the officer's presence. If so, it becomes a "stale misdemeanor." The officer could still cite and release the suspect.

This rule does not require that an officer instantly make an arrest. As long as the officer diligently pursues the investigation it will be held as a valid arrest. Additionally, a violation of this state-imposed rule does not require suppression of evidence or a basis for a civil-right's lawsuit.[1]

Report Writing

If an officer is unable to immediately make an arrest for a misdemeanor committed in their presence, the officer may need to explain the following:

- Articulate that the misdemeanor was committed in your presence;

- Articulate how you diligently pursued the investigation. If you delayed for officer safety reasons (e.g. waited for backup before making a stop);

- Articulate that you did not pursue any other investigations or handle other matters unrelated to the case at hand.

---

[1] Barry v. Fowler, 902 F.2d 770 (9th Cir. Cal. 1990)

Arrest in Public Place

Officers are never required to obtain an arrest warrant when the suspect is located in a public place.[1] A public place would be described as any place where the general public has a right to be.

This rule also applies to places where police are lawfully present, even if not open to the public. For example, police may make a warrantless arrest on a suspect for domestic violence while lawfully investigating the crime inside the home.[2]

REPORT WRITING

1. Articulate how you were <u>lawfully present at the location</u>. If the location is not open to the general public, describe why you were lawfully present:

    a. Inside home during an investigation

    b. Obtained consent by person with apparent authority to enter home or private area of a business

    c. If suspect is outside their front door, you have legal access, and can make the arrest

2. Articulate probable cause for arrest;

3. You may make a search incident to arrest while inside the home;

4. If you go to home or business with intent to make an arrest, make that purpose known *before* you ask to enter.[3]

State law may place restrictions on whether you can make a warrantless arrest for certain offenses.

---

[1] United States v. Watson, 423 U . S. 411 (U . S. 1976)
[2] People v. Patterson, 156 Cal. Rptr. 518 (Cal. App. 2d Dist. 1979)
[3] Toubus v. Superior Court, 114 Cal. App. 3d 378 (Cal. App. 1st Dist. 1981)

Reentry into Home to Make Arrest

This area of the law is not completely settled. We know that undercover officers can summon backup officers to come inside the home to help make the arrest, but generally the undercover officer cannot leave the residence and come back later to make the arrest. If you do decide to leave and immediately reenter with arrest team, articulate an exigency (evidence will be destroyed/sold before warrant). Better yet obtain an anticipatory warrant (for example, the triggering event could be the sale of narcotics).

REPORT WRITING

Articulate the following:

1. The time between leaving and re-entry should be immediate;

2. You should have a good reason for leaving and not making the arrest, officer safety should suffice;

3. If accurate, articulate that there was no time to get a warrant and the need to preserve evidence (seize evidence before sold);

4. Finally, reentry only allows arrest, not search. You would need consent or a search warrant.

SAMPLE LANGUAGE

The key is to articulate that the reentry was immediate.

"On January 1, 2017 Officer Jones, who was undercover as a purchaser of narcotics, was invited into John Doe's residence for a drug transaction. (Describe probable cause for arrest). An arrest team was in the vicinity of Doe's apartment. Officer Jones left Doe's residence at approximately 10:05 p.m., summoned the arrest team, and they immediately reentered at approximately 10:08 p.m. to affect the probable cause arrest of Doe. The reentry was conducted as soon as possible based on the totality of the circumstances." Also, articulate why you chose to leave and come back, versus having the arrest team enter the house while you were present.

CASE EXAMPLES

Additional officers may enter if undercover officer is inside the residence

An informant and undercover police officer went to defendant's residence to arrange a drug transaction. Defendant showed the pair a bag containing cocaine. The pair left the residence and returned with another agent, who was the purported purchaser. The door had been left ajar, so police officers entered the residence and arrested defendant.[1]

Delayed entry unlawful

"In a prosecution arising out of the purchase of stolen weapons from an undercover police officer in defendants' home. Although the undercover officer had been voluntarily admitted into the home, he had walked outside of the house to signal uniformed officers to arrest defendants. The officers then arrested defendants within the house without first obtaining an arrest warrant, seized the weapons sold, and uncovered a rifle in their subsequent search of the house. The court held that despite the legality of the officer's initial entry, his reentry without consent and in the absence of exigent circumstances rendered the arrest and the search incident thereto unlawful."[2]

Immediate reentry lawful

Warrantless arrest of defendant in his residence upheld when defendant had consented to initial entry by police officer, during which time defendant committed crime in officer's presence, after which officer left and immediately reentered with other officers to arrest defendant.[3]

---

[1] Toubus v. Superior Court, 114 Cal. App. 3d 378 (Cal. App. 1st Dist. 1981)
[2] People v. Garcia, 139 Cal. App. 3d Supp. 1 (Cal. App. Dep't Super. Ct. 1982)
[3] People v. Cespedes, 191 Cal. App. 3d 768 (Cal. App. 1st Dist. 1987)

Evidence and 'Non-Arrestable' Offenses

Many states prohibit a custodial arrest for certain offenses. For example, officers may not be allowed to make an arrest for routine traffic violations, or misdemeanor offenses not committed in their presence. Any evidence obtained after such an "unlawful" arrest may be inadmissible in state court.

However, these rules don't apply if the court is applying Fourth Amendment standards for arrests. Further, federal courts are not restricted by state rules. Therefore, even if an arrest violated a state law there would not be a Fourth Amendment violation as long as the arrest was based on probable cause.[1]

GUIDELINES

If you believe the suspect has evidence in their possession, and you cannot make an arrest based on state statutes, you cannot retrieve the evidence without:

1. Consent to search;

2. Search warrant;

3. Legitimate exigency that suspect would destroy the evidence.

---

[1] Devenpeck v. Alford, 543 U.S. 146 (U.S. 2004)

Arrest Based on Mistake of Fact

Generally, evidence will not be suppressed if an officer reasonably relied on a fact that was later proved to be untrue. The exception would be if the mistake of fact was based on deliberate, reckless, or grossly negligent conduct or the result of systemic problems. For example, if an officer relied on a warrant and made an arrest, evidence seized after a search incident to arrest wouldn't be suppressed even if it turned out that the warrant was invalid.[1]

REPORT WRITING

If you conducted a search or arrest based on a fact that was later found to be false or inaccurate, you should articulate how you acted reasonably:

- Based on the facts and circumstances at the time, your belief in the fact was reasonable;

- If the mistake was based on a systemic failure (bad warrant, inaccurate database entry, etc.) articulate that to your knowledge this mistake was isolated and doesn't represent a normal pattern or practice.

---

[1] Herring v. United States, 555 U.S. 135 (U.S. 2009)

When to 'Unarrest' Suspect

There are two situations where you might unarrest a suspect. The first scenario occurs when you arrest a suspect with probable cause, but later find evidence of innocence. Constitutionally you must unarrest the suspect without unreasonable delay. The second scenario occurs when you (or supervisor) decides that continued arrest is not the best outcome for a case. This usually occurs before transportation to jail. As long as the initial arrest had P/C and you acted reasonably (i.e. didn't arrest the person just to conduct a warrantless search or to embarrass the suspect), then it's permitted.

Either way make sure your report is rock solid and fully explain what you did and why you did it. These situations are ripe for lawsuits and are easy money for hungry plaintiff's attorneys.

GUIDELINES

1. It is constitutionally permissible to "unarrest" someone as long as your initial arrest was reasonable and lawful;

2. It is constitutionally required that if you arrest someone and later find evidence that they did not commit the crime (i.e. no longer have probable cause), you must release them. If they are in jail/prison, immediately notify the prosecutor in writing.

'Contempt of Cop' Arrests

Do not make an arrest for "disorderly conduct" or "obstruction" primarily because a person criticizes, insults or challenges your authority. The Supreme Court has made it very clear that they expect law enforcement officers to rise above these insults. They also hold you to a higher standard when it comes to "fighting words."

> "The freedom of individuals to verbally oppose or challenge police action without risking arrest is one of the principal characteristics by which we distinguish a free nation from a police state."[1]

REPORT WRITING

If you make an arrest on a person who also criticized, insulted or challenged you, make sure that your report focuses on the legitimacy of the arrest, not any "contempt of cop" type remarks.

CASE EXAMPLES

Officer criminalized First Amendment speech

Suspect yelled "Why don't you pick on somebody your own size?" while his friend was getting arrested. When officer asked if he was interfering with his duties, suspected yelled, "Why don't you pick on someone my size!" Suspect was arrested for obstruction. Court held the arrest was unlawful and police cannot criminalize First Amendment speech.[2]

---

[1] Houston v. Hill, 482 U.S. 451 (U.S. 1987)
[2] Id.

Freedom of Speech & Public Protests

Generally, be very hesitant before you take any enforcement action against a person or group who appears to be exercising their rights under the First Amendment. Courts are very quick to come down on officers who violate a person's freedom of speech.

Officers usually cannot regulate the content of a person's speech, just the time, place and manner.[1] For example, if a group was loudly protesting in a residential neighborhood at two in the morning, it would be permissible to order that they move their protest to the main city park, away from sleeping residents.

REPORT WRITING

Governments can regulate the time, place and manner of protests. However, these rules must be content neutral and apply equally to all groups. If police need to regulate a protest they should first seek consent, if that fails, and there's no immediate safety concern, consult with legal counsel.

If legal counsel is unavailable or there's a legitimate safety or disturbance of the peace issue, articulate how the police order was limited to time, place or manner restrictions.

---

[1] Snyder v. Phelps, 562 U.S. 443 (U.S. 2011)

Search Incident to Arrest

You have automatic authority to conduct full searches (except strip/cavity searches) of a person after they have been lawfully arrested.[1] You may also search any items the person is going to bring with them to jail.

If you are going to take other property and store it for safekeeping, you can conduct an inventory.

GUIDELINES

You may conduct a search incident to arrest even if you don't believe the suspect has contraband or evidence. The search should be conducted contemporaneously with the arrest (the sooner the better). Any evidence found will be admissible in court.

The court outlined three reasons for these searches:

1. To discover weapons or other contraband;

2. To discover evidence (if pertinent to the charged offense); and

3. To discover any means of escape.

SAMPLE LANGUAGE

"After arresting Doe I conducted a search incident to arrest. I did not discover any contraband, evidence, or means of escape."

"I conducted a search incident to arrest and discovered a small baggie containing a crystalline substance which I believed to be methamphetamine inside Doe's wallet."

---

[1] Chimel v. Cal., 395 U.S. 752 (U.S. 1969)

Search Incident to 'Temporary' Arrest

Sometimes you'll make an arrest with the intention to later "release" the suspect at another location. For example, you may arrest a juvenile with the intent to release him to his parents. Or you may take a person into civil custody for public intoxication with the intent to transport him to the hospital. Even under these conditions you may make a full search incident to arrest primarily for officer safety reasons.

GUIDELINES

1. You may conduct a search incident to arrest even if you don't plan to formally book the suspect; but

2. Some type of suspect transportation is usually required.

This rule doesn't apply if you plan to "cite and release" a suspect on-scene.[1]

CASE EXAMPLES

Transporting truant juvenile back to school was an arrest

An officer stopped a truant juvenile several miles from school. After determining that the student was indeed skipping class, the officer searched the teen before transporting him back to school. A dagger was found and the teen argued it was an unlawful search. The court disagreed, and said that the teen was technically arrested, even though the result was school, not jail. Therefore, the search was incident to a lawful arrest.[2] Note, the key point in this case was the way California law classified this law. Some states may not classify truancy as a crime per se.

---

[1] Knowles v. Iowa, 525 U.S. 113 (U.S. 1998)
[2] In re Humberto O., 80 Cal. App. 4th 237 (Cal. App. 2d Dist. 2000)

Search Before Arrest

Generally, there is no prohibition in making a pre-arrest "patsearch" of a subject right before you formally arrest them (compare to "patdown," which is only for weapons). The Supreme Court requires that a search incident to lawful arrest be conducted "contemporaneously."[1] This means the search could occur *before* the formal arrest (though not common).

GUIDELINES

Consider the following before conducting a search *before* arrest:

1. You must have P/C to make the arrest *before* the search;

2. You should have P/C that the suspect currently possesses the evidence you seek (e.g. drugs, stolen property, etc.);

3. The conduct of your search must be reasonable.

CASE EXAMPLES

Searches must be "contemporaneous" with the arrest

"The fact defendant is not formally arrested until after the search does not invalidate the search if probable cause to arrest exists prior to the search and the search is substantially contemporaneous with the arrest."[2]

If officer develops P/C during patdown, he can conduct full search

"However, an officer may reach into clothing to recover items that do not feel like weapons when the officer has probable cause to arrest the suspect. At that point, the patdown may be expanded to a full search permitted incident to arrest."[3]

---

[1] Chimel v. Cal., 395 U.S. 752 (U.S. 1969)
[2] People v. Adams, 175 Cal. App. 3d 855 (Cal. App. 2d Dist. 1985)
[3] People v. Collins, 2011 Cal. App. Unpub. LEXIS 5863 (Cal. App. 3d Dist. Aug. 4, 2011)

Search of Property After Arrest

Whenever you conduct a search incident to arrest, it should be done *contemporaneously* with the arrest.[1] Generally, this means the search should be conducted during the same time and location as the arrest. If you conduct the search later at the jail you should have a reason. For example, during a hot call you couldn't conduct the search of property on-scene. Try to stay away from *double searches* where you search on-scene and again at jail. Courts will look at this more as a fishing expedition, not a legitimate exception to the warrant requirement.[2]

GUIDELINES

A search incident to arrest should be done at the same time and location as the arrest. If search of property is done at the jail or police station have a reason (officer safety, inventory, etc.). If you don't have a good reason the search may not be deemed "contemporaneous" with arrest and any evidence found may (though not likely) be suppressed at trial.

Note, many courts are becoming much more relaxed about contemporaneous searches that are incident to arrest. But still know that this is generally the rule.

SAMPLE LANGUAGE

"I searched Doe's person incident to arrest. However, because there was still an outstanding violent suspect I was unable to search Doe's property on-scene because of officer safety concerns. I continued my search incident to arrest of Doe's backpack at jail and discovered... ."

[1] Chimel v. Cal., 395 U.S. 752 (U.S. 1969)
[2] New York v. Belton, 453 U.S. 454 (U.S. 1981)

'Hot Pursuit' Versus 'Fresh Pursuit'

There's a difference between "hot pursuit" and "fresh pursuit." Hot pursuit is when you're literally chasing a suspect who is trying to flee. You can follow him anywhere he goes, and it doesn't matter if the crime was a misdemeanor. Fresh pursuit, on the other hand, is where you have identified a suspect in a *violent* felony and are actively tracking him down. Once you find out where he's hiding you can usually make a warrantless entry and arrest him. If it's a non-violent crime, get a warrant.

GUIDELINES

Hot pursuit: You're allowed to chase after a suspect who runs into a house, even if the crime is a misdemeanor;[1]

Fresh pursuit: If you're actively tracking down a violent felon, you can make a warrantless entry in order to make the arrest. However, this warrant exception is not valid forever. After about three hours you're probably pushing it.[2]

---

[1] People v. Lloyd, 216 Cal. App. 3d 1425 (Cal. App. 2d Dist. 1989)
[2] Minnesota v. Olson, 495 U.S. 91 (U.S. 1990)

Fresh Pursuit

Fresh pursuit occurs whenever police respond to a violent crime (e.g. murder, rape, armed robbery) and investigators are hot on the suspect's trail.[1]

REPORT WRITING

Articulate the following:

1. Describe the crime and probable cause to make the arrest;

2. Articulate why the suspect presented a danger if not immediately apprehended. Also, if appropriate, articulate that there was perishable evidence on the suspect that must be secured without delay (gunshot residue, semen, blood, clothing);

3. Describe how your pursuit of the suspect was immediate and continuous after the crime (more than 3 hours is pushing it);

4. Articulate why the suspect is currently inside the residence;[2]

5. Knock and announce rules apply, unless doing so would be dangerous (shouldn't be an issue under most circumstances);

Plain view applies, but you need a warrant to *search* for evidence.

CASE EXAMPLES

Officers were in fresh pursuit of murder suspect 2 ½ hours later

Where there was a 2 1/2 investigation between a robbery-murder and the location of the defendant's home, the officers were found to be in "fresh pursuit," justifying a warrantless entry to look for the suspect.[3]

---

[1] Minnesota v. Olson, 495 U.S. 91 (U.S. 1990)
[2] People v. Wader, 5 Cal. 4th 610 (Cal. 1993)
[3] People v. Gilbert, 63 Cal. 2d 690 (Cal. 1965)

Hot Pursuit

We often chase after fleeing suspects (it's good exercise). Sometimes suspects try to retreat into a residence and hot pursuit allows you to chase after them in order to make the arrest.[1] For safety reasons you don't have to immediately follow the suspect inside the home, you're allowed wait for backup and then make "hot pursuit entry."[2]

REPORT WRITING

1. Describe what crimes the suspect committed before entering a home (traffic offense, resisting arrest, eluding, etc.);

2. Describe why you reasonably believed the subject was inside the residence. Usually you'll see the subject run into the residence, other times you'll develop facts or circumstances that identify his location. For example, you observe a suspect flee his vehicle after crashing into a light pole and he escapes. You run his license plate and the registered address is only two blocks away. You arrive at the address five minutes later and see the suspect's jacket inside his trash can. It would be reasonable to make a warrantless hot pursuit entry and arrest the suspect. Best practice: get a warrant.

- Plain view applies, but you need a warrant to search for evidence.

CASE EXAMPLE

Officers can pursue suspect fleeing from infraction

Officers may even pursue a person into his home upon attempting to cite him for an infraction where the suspect flees into his home. The defendant's resistance converts the offense into a misdemeanor "resisting arrest."[3]

---

[1] People v. Lloyd, 216 Cal. App. 3d 1425 (Cal. App. 2d Dist. 1989)
[2] In re Lavoyne M., 221 Cal. App. 3d 154 (Cal. App. 4th Dist. 1990)
[3] People v. Lloyd, 216 Cal. App. 3d 1425 (Cal. App. 2d Dist. 1989)

Investigations

Collective Knowledge Doctrine

The collective knowledge doctrine is one of the most powerful and important doctrines in law enforcement. It allows a single police officer to benefit from the collective knowledge of all officers working on a case. For example, if a detective asks another officer to search a suitcase for drugs. the search would be valid even if the officer conducting the search had no idea why he was authorized to search the suitcase, as long as the detective had probable cause or consent.

The key with the collective knowledge doctrine is that officers communicate with each other. This doesn't mean officers have to know everything about the case, but they at least have to be working together.

REPORT WRITING

Articulate the following:

1. Indicate in your report that you had some <u>degree of communication</u> with other officers;

2. And this communication concerned the <u>current</u> investigation.

CASE EXAMPLES

Collective knowledge doctrine applied to officer who stopped vehicle

A narcotics task force requested that an officer stop a vehicle for any observed traffic violation. Though the arresting officer only observed a traffic offense, the collective knowledge of the task force permitted the later arrest and warrantless search of the vehicle for drugs.[1]

---

[1] United States v. Thompson, 533 F.3d 964 (8th Cir. Mo. 2008)

Anonymous Tips

Police often receive anonymous tips, especially through 911. These calls often state that a particular driver is either drunk or reckless. Often, you can use these tips to establish reasonable suspicion, even though the caller remains anonymous or otherwise refuses to get involved.

REPORT WRITING

If you're going to act on an anonymous tip, articulate the following:[1]

1. Amount of detail provided (especially details that the general public would not know);

2. Whether future behavior was accurately predicted;

3. Whether information was corroborated (see next section);

4. Whether the information is based on first-hand observations;

5. Whether the tip came through 911 or face-to-face (this helps)

6. Whether the source was involved in illegal conduct and they are taking a legal risk or sacrificing their safety by providing information to police; and

7. The timeliness of the report (the more recent the better because the informant has less time to create a lie).

---

[1] Navarette v. California, 134 S. Ct. 1683 (U.S. 2014)

Corroboration of Anonymous Tips

Typically, if you want to use an anonymous tip to make a reasonable suspicion stop you have to corroborate the information. Essentially, this means confirming that the information given is true.

REPORT WRITING

Articulate as much of the following as possible:[1]

1. An accurate prediction of a suspect's future activity (i.e., "predictive information") by the tipster;

2. Seemingly innocent activity when the anonymous tip casts the activity in a suspicious light;

3. Suspect is in a "high crime area;"

4. Verification of details through police observation or other sources;

5. If appropriate, articulate that even though the tipster remained anonymous, they could be held accountable for providing false information to the police:[2]

6. The ability of authorities to identify the informant;

7. The consequences the informant is likely to experience as a result of providing false information; and

8. The informant's understanding that they may be criminally charged if found to have lied to police.

---

[1] People v. Ramirez, 41 Cal. App. 4th 1608 (Cal. App. 4th Dist. 1996)
[2] People v. Jordan, 121 Cal. App. 4th 544 (Cal. App. 5th Dist. 2004)

Confidential Informants

If you use a confidential informant (C/I) to establish reasonable suspicion or probable cause, you need to articulate he was trustworthy. Articulate how the C/I was "credible" and how he obtained his "basis of knowledge."[1]

Credible means that the C/I was telling the truth. Basis of knowledge means that the information shared by the C/I was accurate, usually because of first-hand observations.[2]

REPORT WRITING

Describe how the C/I was credible:

1. Made statements against penal interest

2. Provided reliable information in the past

3. C/I was not a criminal, but an upstanding citizen

4. C/I was a criminal, but met face to face (extra weight because C/I is exposing himself to arrest and officer can judge C/I's demeanor[3]

Describe C/I's basis of knowledge:

5. C/I saw contraband or evidence first-hand

6. Information accurately predicted future conduct

7. Information was corroborated with other sources

8. C/I had extensive experience in the criminal enterprise, and was able to "put the pieces" together

9. Finally, state that based on the totality of the circumstances, the C/I's information contributed to R/S or P/C.

---

[1] Aguilar v. Tex., 378 U.S. 108 (U.S. 1964)
[2] Illinois v. Gates, 462 U.S. 213 (U.S. 1983)
[3] United States v. Palos-Marquez, 591 F.3d 1272 (9th Cir. Cal. 2010)

Recording Video Inside Homes

A suspect has no reasonable expectation of privacy in the information they voluntarily expose to undercover officers or government agents (i.e. confidential informants). Therefore, police may secretly record video and audio while inside a home and use those recordings in a search warrant.

GUIDELINES

There is no Fourth Amendment violation if police or their agents secretly record video and/or video while lawfully present inside a home. Also, uniformed officers may record using body-cams.

CASE EXAMPLES

Informants may wear video and audio recorders

Defendant argued that secretly recording video and audio of his private conversation with an undercover agent violated his reasonable expectation of privacy. The court held otherwise, and said that the recordings revealed no more than what the defendant said and did in front of the agent.[1]

No privacy when speaking in a foreign language not understood by informant

An undercover informant recorded his conversation with the target, and another accomplice. When the target did not want the informant to understand what he was saying to the other accomplice, he would speak Spanish. These conversations were later translated. Court held there was no reasonable expectation of privacy in these conversations.[2]

[1] United States v. Wahchumwah, 710 F.3d 862 (9th Cir. Wash. 2013)
[2] United States v. Longoria, 177 F.3d 1179 (10th Cir. Kan. 1999)

Identifications

Courts are scrutinizing police identification procedures more than they have in the past. One reason is because research has shown that eyewitnesses are easily swayed by suggestive practices. For example, if police make an investigative detention on a potential armed robbery suspect, it would be improper to say to the victim, "We have the suspect, but we still need you to ID him."

It's vital that police stay as neutral and detached as possible when it comes to identification procedures.[1]

REPORT WRITING

Articulate the following:

1. Witness' ability to see the crime;

2. Witness' focal attention;

3. Accuracy of witness' description prior to capture/identification;

4. Level of certainty displayed by witness during identification;

5. Length of time between crime and identification;

6. Describe how police minimized any suggestive influences.

---

[1] Neil v. Biggers, 409 U.S. 188 (U.S. 1972)

'Show-Ups'

Police may conduct a one-on-one "show-up" between the suspect and witness under a few circumstances.[1] Usually, these show-ups are conducted soon after the crime has occurred when police have detained a suspect (on-scene or in the vicinity).

Whenever you conduct any kind of identification procedure it's important that you don't use words or conduct that's overly suggestive.

REPORT WRITING

Articulate the following:

1. Witness' ability to see the crime;

2. Witness' focal attention;

3. Accuracy of witness' description prior to identification;

4. Words used by police to minimize suggestive influences;

5. Staging the suspect should not give appearance of guilt:

    a. Location of suspect (shouldn't be in back of patrol car)

    b. Few officers immediately near suspect

    c. Whether handcuffs were used, if so why (combative, etc.)

    d. Suspect's physical/emotional condition

6. Level of certainty displayed by witness during identification;

7. Length of time between crime and identification;

8. Describe how police minimized any suggestive influences (words and conduct)

---

[1] Neil v. Biggers, 409 U.S. 188 (U.S. 1972)

Voice & Writing Samples

The Fifth Amendment prohibits compelling a person from testifying against himself and does not apply to physical evidence. Voice and writing samples are considered physical evidence, like fingerprints.

Police are allowed to gather voice and writing samples just like any other evidence. For example, if police conduct a lawful search and see writing samples, they may seize them as evidence (if appropriate to the case). Similarly, if a suspect makes a recorded jailhouse call the recording can be compared with other voice samples. If necessary, get a search warrant to compel a suspect to provide a voice or writing sample (refusal can be used in court).

REPORT WRITING

If you use a voice or writing sample, focus on the "physical" elements of the evidence, not the testimonial nature of the sample. For example, if you wanted a suspect to repeat the words used in an extortion case, you couldn't argue that since the defendant said the same words, he admitted to the extortion. But if you played the recording to the victim, they could testify that the voice was the same or similar to the one originally heard.

CASE EXAMPLES

Court upheld voice comparisons

> The defendant was booked into jail. His booking question interview was recorded and his voice was compared to recordings from an authorized wiretap. The voices matched. Court found that defendant had no reasonable expectation of privacy in his voice.[1]

---

[1] United States v. Ceballos, 385 F.3d 1120 (7th Cir. Ind. 2004)

Interview & Interrogation

Inherent Reliability of Witnesses & Victims

Often when you investigate a crime, you will talk to various witnesses and victims. The Supreme Court has held that these citizens are presumed to be reliable, unlike a criminal confidential informant.[1]

GUIDELINES

Because citizen witnesses and victims are presumptively reliable, you have no obligation to examine further the basis of the witness' knowledge or talk with any other witness. Obviously, this doesn't relieve you of conducting a quality investigation that seeks the truth.

CASE EXAMPLE

Police don't need to be skeptical about citizen witnesses

"We begin by noting that when examining informant evidence used to support a claim of probable cause for a warrant, or a warrantless arrest, the skepticism and careful scrutiny usually found in cases involving informants, sometimes anonymous, from the criminal milieu, is appropriately relaxed if the informant is an identified victim or ordinary citizen witness."[2]

Witness not unreliable just because they were intoxicated

"Although it is possible that an angry and intoxicated person may be less reliable than a detached uninterested observer who is sober, it is equally possible that those same factors can make a witness more inclined to be truthful than they otherwise might."[3]

---

[1] Illinois v. Gates, 462 U.S. 213 (U.S. 1983)
[2] Easton v. Boulder, 776 F.2d 1441 (10th Cir. Colo. 1985)
[3] Hale v. Kart, 396 F.3d 721 (6th Cir. Mich. 2005)

De Facto Interrogations

An arrest occurs when a reasonable person believes they are "in-custody." It doesn't matter what police "think:" It only matters what they do and say. If courts determine a "de-facto" arrest occurred Miranda would be required.

GUIDELINES

Courts consider the following:[1]

1. Whether the suspect was told he was free to leave;

2. Suspect was not under formal arrest;

3. The suspect could move about freely during questions;

4. Suspect voluntarily responded to questioning;

5. Whether environment was "police-dominated;"

6. Whether police use strong-arm tactics or deception; and

7. Whether police arrested the suspect at the termination of interview.

CASE EXAMPLES

Subjective intentions don't matter

An individual is deemed "in custody" where there has been a formal arrest, or where there has been a restraint on freedom of movement of the degree associated with a formal arrest so that a reasonable person would not feel free to leave. A suspect's or the police's subjective view of the circumstances does not determine whether the suspect is in custody.[2]

---

[1] State v. Taylor, 968 P.2d 315 (Nev. 1998)
[2] Stansbury v. Cal., 511 U.S. 318 (U.S. 1994)

How to Minimize Coercive Influences

You may unintentionally create a coercive environment when you detain a suspect. For example, you may need to draw your firearm or use handcuffs for safety purposes. If you intend to obtain a voluntary statement you should minimize those coercive influences and articulate your actions in your report.

GUIDELINES

Do the following, and articulate these in your report:

- Use "conversational" language;

- Explain to the suspect why guns were drawn or handcuffs were used. If you can later remove handcuffs, do so;

- Tell the suspect that they are not under arrest (important);

- Offer bathroom breaks;

- If appropriate offer the suspect snacks, water or coffee;

- If suspect is mentally defective, use simple language.

Courts tend to ignore the inherent coerciveness of a police uniform and/or badge, and the fact that most people are reluctant to ignore a police officer's questions.

When Miranda is Required

Two requirements must be met before you're required tell a suspect their Miranda rights. And if both requirements don't exist at the same time, then Miranda is not required. The requirements are the suspect must be "in-custody" and you must "interrogate" them.[1]

GUIDELINES

In-custody: You don't need to formally tell someone they are under arrest for them to be in-custody. The courts will look at whether an objectively reasonable person would have believed they were under arrest based on the totality of the circumstances, even if you never intended to arrest them (referred to as a de facto arrest).

Interrogation: Whenever you seek "testimony" from a person who's in custody, Miranda is required. Basically, testimony are statements which tend to prove, or disprove, the crime in question. Booking-type questions don't count.

A suspect cannot pre-invoke Miranda. For example, if you arrest a suspect and he says, "I want my lawyer!," but you haven't even started to interrogate him, then it's not a valid invocation.

---

[1] Miranda v. Ariz., 384 U.S. 436 (U.S. 1966)

Report Writing

1. If the suspect tries to pre-invoke articulate in your report that one of the requirements were not present, i.e. they were not in custody or if they were in-custody, you were not interrogating them;

2. You don't have to read Miranda if you don't interrogate the arrestee. If the arrestee makes incriminating comments they would be admissible as long as it wasn't in response to investigation-related questioning (i.e. uncoerced utterances);

1. If you ask booking-type questions (name, date of birth, etc.) then Miranda is unnecessary.

2. Miranda is required even if you're interrogating the suspect about an unrelated crime. If they are in custody for any offense, then Miranda is required for any interrogation. There is an exception for prisoners. See next section.

Case Examples

Miranda not necessarily required after detaining a suspect with handcuffs

"Handcuffing a suspect during an investigative detention does not automatically make it (a) custodial interrogation for purposes of Miranda."[1]

Temporarily placing suspect in patrol car not an arrest

Handcuffing and putting an uncooperative suspect in the backseat of a patrol car while the officer checked the vehicle for weapons held not to be an arrest. "A brief, although complete, restriction of liberty, such as handcuffing (and, in this case, putting into a patrol car), during a Terry stop is not a de facto arrest, if not excessive under the circumstances."[2]

---

[1] People v. Davidson, 221 Cal. App. 4th 966 (Cal. App. 2d Dist. 2013)
[2] Haynie v. County of L.A., 339 F.3d 1071 (9th Cir. Cal. 2003)

Miranda in Jails & Prisons

Interviewing a suspect in jail or prison about an unrelated crime doesn't necessarily mean they are in custody for Miranda purposes. Courts will look at several factors. Still, a good rule of thumb is to read Miranda for jail inmates and it's optional for prison inmates. This is because jail is not a person's home and therefore they are usually in-custody for Miranda purposes. However, courts typically view prisons as quasi-homes for inmates, and therefore not "per se" in-custody.

Guidelines

Follow these rules:

If interviewing a jail inmate read the suspect their Miranda warnings. An exception would be where the inmate has been sentenced and is serving their time in the jail. Best practice is to read Miranda;

If interviewing a prison inmate, you do not typically have to read Miranda. But your actions should not be more "restrictive or coercive" than typical for the prison environment. If a locked interview room is used tell them they are free to leave at any time (after getting the guard to take them back to their cell).[1]

---

[1] Miranda v. Ariz., 384 U.S. 436 (U.S. 1966)

Miranda in Schools

Miranda is not required if the school is investigating a violation of school policy or instructs the student to empty their pockets. However, if the school is conducting primarily a criminal investigation, or a SRO or police officer is present, Miranda will be required if the student is in custody and being interrogated.

CASE EXAMPLES

Miranda not required for drug investigation

A vice-principle interrogating a student about drug possession was not required to Mirandize the student, even though police were called but had not arrived. However, once the officer arrived, continued interrogation without Miranda would be a violation.[1]

Some states require parental notification

Keep in mind that some states also require that the student's parents be notified before conducting an interrogation.[2]

Dean not required to give Miranda before ordering student to empty pockets

A dean received information that a student possessed narcotics. The dean confronted the student and ordered him to empty his pockets, which revealed narcotics. Police were called and the student was arrested. Court held that dean was acting as an educator, not agent of law enforcement and no Miranda required.[3]

---

[1] People v. Pankhurst, 365 Ill. App. 3d 248 (Ill. App. Ct. 2d Dist. 2006)
[2] State v. M.A.L., 1988 OK CR 274 (Okla. Crim. App. 1988)
[3] People v. Stewart, 63 Misc. 2d 601 (N.Y. City Crim. Ct. 1970)

Invocation Prior to Interrogation

A suspect cannot "pre-invoke" his Miranda rights. He must wait for you to start the interrogation process before invoking his rights.[1]

GUIDELINES

Sometimes a person will try to invoke their Miranda rights before you even try to talk to them. Generally, you can ignore that invocation until you're ready to actually interrogate the suspect. Of course, you will need to tell them their Miranda rights and receive a knowing and intelligent waiver.

CASE EXAMPLES

Suspect's demand for a lawyer during non-custodial interview was not a Miranda invocation

A murder suspect named Archie Dixon walked into a police station to retrieve his car which had been impounded for traffic violations. When a homicide detective happened to see him, the detective decided to use the opportunity to question him about the murder. But Dixon refused to answer any questions unless his lawyer was present. A few days later, having developed probable cause, the detective arrested Dixon and, after Mirandizing him, obtained an incriminating statement. The Supreme Court held that since Dixon wasn't under arrest when he initially demanded a lawyer, his later Miranda waiver was valid.[2]

---

[1] McNeil v. Wis., 501 U.S. 171 (U.S. 1991)
[2] Bobby v. Dixon, 132 S. Ct. 26 (U.S. 2011)

Miranda Warning Elements

The following Miranda warnings are required when you interrogate a suspect in-custody.[1] Additionally, you must read a suspect their entire Miranda rights, even if they cut you off and tell you they already know their rights.[2] This is true even if you arrested a judge! All warnings

GUIDELINES

Articulate the following elements:

1. He has the right to remain silent;

2. That any statements made may be used as evidence against him;

3. That he has the right to consult with an attorney and to have that attorney present during questioning;

4. That if he cannot afford an attorney, one will be appointed to represent him prior to questioning;

5. The suspect must *knowingly* and *intelligently* waive rights.

Note: Courts don't require these rights to be read verbatim.[3] But police must inform the suspect of all four and articulate the fifth. It's highly suggested that you read Miranda from a pre-printed pocket card, otherwise be prepared to be slammed in court by a decent defense attorney because you don't know *exactly* what you said to the defendant.

---

[1] Miranda v. Ariz., 384 U.S. 436 (U.S. 1966)
[2] United States v. Patane, 542 U.S. 630 (U.S. 2004)
[3] Florida v. Powell, 559 U.S. 50 (U.S. 2010)

Right to Remain Silent Versus Request for Lawyer

After you tell a person their Miranda rights they can essentially tell you one of three things:

1. I want to talk;

2. I don't want to talk;

3. I want a lawyer.

Number 1 is a waiver, and numbers' 2 and 3 are Miranda invocations.

GUIDELINES

If a person invokes their right to remain silent, you must stop the questioning. However, after an appropriate "cooling off" period you may try again for a waiver;

If a person invokes their right to counsel, you must stop all questioning while the person is in custody. If they are released from custody, you can approach the suspect again after 14 days has passed (without giving Miranda because now there is no custody).

Re-engagement After Invocation to Remain Silent

If you begin the interrogation process, and the suspect tells you he does not want to talk, you must not ask him anymore questions. The only exception would be public safety questions and routine booking questions. However, the Supreme Court said that after a "significant period of time" you may reengage the suspect and seek a knowing and intelligent waiver as long as you "scrupulously honored" suspect's invocation (left him alone).

GUIDELINES

Right to remain silent: Once a suspect invokes this right all questioning must immediately cease. However, you can further question him after an appropriate "cooling off" period. The Supreme Court found that a two-hour period was sufficient.[1]

CASE EXAMPLES

Two-hour break, along with Miranda waiver, found to be sufficient

"After an interval of more than two hours, Mosley was questioned by another police officer at another location about an unrelated holdup murder. He was given full and complete *Miranda* warnings at the outset of the second interrogation. He was thus reminded again that he could remain silent and could consult with a lawyer, and was carefully given a full and fair opportunity to exercise these options."[2] Suspect gave a valid waiver.

---

[1] Michigan v. Mosley, 423 U.S. 96 (U.S. 1975)
[2] Id.

Re-engagement After Invocation to Right to Counsel

When a suspect invokes their right to counsel, the interrogation must stop and there's no "cooling off" period while in custody. However, there is a rule that may allow you try again after the suspect has been released from custody.

GUIDELINE

Right to counsel: If the suspect invokes their right to counsel all questioning must stop. If he's released, then his previous invocation is valid for 14 days from the day he is released.[1] This right is not "crime" specific and all questioning must cease.

CASE EXAMPLES

All questioning must cease if a suspect invokes right to counsel

"When an accused has invoked his right to have counsel present during a custodial interrogation, a valid waiver of that right cannot be established by showing only that he responded to further police-initiated custodial interrogation even if he has been advised of his rights. An accused, having expressed his desire to deal with the police only through counsel, is not subject to further interrogation by the authorities until counsel has been made available to him, unless the accused himself initiates further communication, exchanges, or conversations with the police."[2]

---

[1] Maryland v. Shatzer, 559 U.S. 98 (U.S. 2010)
[2] Edwards v. Ariz., 451 U.S. 477 (U.S. 1981)

Public Safety Exception

Miranda warnings are not required if you're asking legitimate public safety questions.[1] The safety concern must be something that is pressing, and will likely cause substantial bodily harm or death.

REPORT WRITING

Public Safety Exception: You may ask suspect questions that concern legitimate public safety. For example, you arrest an active shooter and want to know if he planted any bombs, or you arrest an armed robber and ask where the gun is.

Appropriate questions may include:

1. Did you plant any more bombs?

2. Do you know of any other victims?

3. Are there any other weapons or explosives?

4. Where did you hide the gun? (If public would get ahold of it.)

CASE EXAMPLES

Police lawfully asked suspect where he ditched the gun

> The Supreme Court crafted an exception to Miranda for situations where a suspect's silence may imminently endanger the public or police. After cornering a rape suspect in a supermarket, police found that the suspect, reported to be armed, was wearing an empty holster. Without first giving him Miranda warnings, police asked him where he had ditched the gun. He responded, "the gun is over there," and gestured toward a stack of empty cartons. Behind the cartons, police found a loaded revolver and his admission was admitted against him at trial.[2]

[1] New York v. Quarles, 467 U.S. 649 (U.S. 1984)
[2] United States v. Peace, 2014 U.S. Dist. LEXIS 169455 (N.D. Ga. Sept. 25, 2014)

Routine Booking Questions

Miranda warnings are not required if you're asking routine booking questions.[1]

REPORT WRITING

Routine Booking Information: Police may ask routine biological information in order to complete booking and pre-trial services. However, if the information is not needed for booking, and would likely produce an incriminating response, it's considered interrogation.

CASE EXAMPLES

Questions about where suspect worked not booking question

The suspect was arrested after he solicited sex from an underage teenager on the internet. During an interrogation, he invoked his right to counsel twice. Subsequently, the detective asked him various questions from the booking sheet, including where he worked. This information was used at trial. The court of appeals found this was a Miranda violation, and suppressed the evidence.[2]

A request for basic information is not interrogation

A request for routine information necessary for basic identification purposes is not interrogation under Miranda, even if the information turns out to be incriminating. Only if the government agent should reasonably be aware that the information sought...is directly relevant to the offense charged, will the question be subject to scrutiny.[3]

---

[1] Pa. v. Muniz, 496 U.S. 582 (U.S. 1990)
[2] United States v. Hart, 2009 U.S. Dist. LEXIS 72473 (W.D. Ky. Aug. 17, 2009)
[3] United States v. Johnson, 2008 U.S. Dist. LEXIS 110421 (D.S.D. July 10, 2008)

Miranda Violations

Sometimes you'll mistakenly interrogate a suspect without Miranda. If this happens then naturally that testimony cannot be used. Courts separate the violations into two categories, intentional and unintentional violations. Depending on which rule you violated, you may still be able to obtain a valid Miranda waiver.

Guidelines

Intentional violations: If you intentionally interrogate a suspect without Miranda as a tactic to gain a confession, or coerce the suspect, it will not matter that you later obtained a waiver, both confessions will be excluded;[1]

Unintentional violations: If you accidently fail to Mirandize you may be able to obtain a valid waiver later.[2] Courts will want to see that you "cleansed" the invalid interrogation. Here are some suggestions:

1. Advise suspect that previous testimony cannot be used;

2. Have new officer conduct second interrogation;

3. Change locations;

4. Allow some time to pass before taking second statement;

5. You must provide a fresh Miranda warning and receive a knowing and intelligent waiver.

---

[1] Missouri v. Seibert, 542 U.S. 600 (U.S. 2004)
[2] Or. v. Elstad, 470 U.S. 298 (U.S. 1985)

Evidence Found as a Result of Miranda Violation

The exclusionary rule doesn't apply to technical Miranda violations, when the suspect wasn't coerced or compelled to speak.

Guidelines

The Exclusionary rule applies to Fourth Amendment violations, and Miranda is a Fifth Amendment right. Therefore, if a police officer interrogates a suspect without obtaining a Miranda waiver then only the testimony cannot be used. Any evidence found as a result of the testimony may be admitted at trial.

Remember, the seizure of any evidence must be done legally and this type of conduct is highly discouraged. In fact, the 9th Circuit has allowed lawsuits against police officers who intentional violate Miranda.[1]

Additionally, flagrant conduct by officers could be viewed as a Due Process violation, subject to a civil rights lawsuit and suppression of evidence. Do not use this as evidence-gathering tactic.

Case Examples

Miranda does not apply to evidence

> The core protection afforded by the Fifth Amendment, is a prohibition on compelling a defendant to testify against himself at trial. The Clause cannot be violated by the introduction of nontestimonial evidence obtained as a result of voluntary statements.[2]

---

[1] Cooper v. Dupnik, 963 F.2d 1220 (9th Cir. Ariz. 1992)
[2] United States v. Patane, 542 U.S. 630 (U.S. 2004)

Ambiguous Invocations

If a suspect intends to invoke their rights, they must do so clearly, directly and unambiguously. (You're not a mind reader for God sakes!) Suspects that merely mention abstract ideas about their rights will not be viewed as actually invoking them. For example, if a suspect says, "Maybe I should get a lawyer." That's ambiguous and a reasonable person would not take that to mean the suspect wants a lawyer, but is merely thinking about getting one. Therefore, you could keep asking questions.

Report Writing

Articulate the following:

1. Whenever a suspect makes an ambiguous request for a lawyer, try to record their statement word for word and the way they said it in your report, including any follow-up comments you made.

2. Articulate why you thought their statement was not an invocation. For example, imagine a suspect laughed and asked, "You know any good lawyers in town?" You would articulate that a reasonable person would believe the suspect was joking (by laughing) and how you thought he asked a rhetorical question and didn't really expect an answer.

Case Examples

Suspect must clearly invoke his rights

"The suspect must unambiguously request counsel. A statement either is such an assertion of the right to counsel or it is not...he must articulate his desire to have counsel present sufficiently clearly that a reasonable police officer in the circumstances would understand the statement to be a request for an attorney." [1]

---

[1] Davis v. United States, 114 S. Ct. 2350 (U.S. 1994)

Suspect Decides to Talk

If a suspect invokes their Miranda rights, questioning must cease. However, it's possible for a suspect to change their mind after invocation if you keep the below guidelines in mind.[1]

REPORT WRITING

Articulate the following:

- The suspect's decision to initiate questioning was made freely, not as a result of badgering or coercion; and

- It reasonably appeared that the suspect wanted to open up a general discussion about the crime, as opposed to merely discussing unrelated matters or "routine incidents of the custodial relationship."

- Reread Miranda and get an express waiver.

CASE EXAMPLES

Suspect must initiate further communication with police

"An accused who requests an attorney, having expressed his desire to deal with the police only through counsel, is not subject to further interrogation by the authorities until counsel has been made available to him, unless the accused himself initiates further communication, exchanges, or conversations with the police.[2]

---

[1] People v. Davis, 46 Cal. 4th 539 (Cal. 2009)
[2] Minnick v. Mississippi, 498 U.S. 146 (U.S. 1990)

Miranda Re-Advisements

Generally, you don't have to "remind" a suspect of their Miranda rights during interrogation. If the suspect gave a knowing and intelligent waiver once, you're usually fine. However, during some complicated investigations the waiver may become "stale" and therefore courts may want to see follow-up waivers.

GUIDELINES

Consider a re-advisement under the following conditions:

1. A lot of time has passed between the waiver and suspect's statement;

2. Significant interruptions in the continuity of investigation;

3. Change in locations;

4. Different officers interview the suspect; and

5. Whether the suspect has later changed their testimony.

CASE EXAMPLES

Asking suspect if he remembered Miranda upheld

"Where defendant voluntarily appeared at police station to inquire of shooting and...led officer to believe that defendant's involvement was more than casual curiosity and thereupon officer read defendant's rights from a "Miranda card" after which defendant was questioned briefly and remained in station until investigation shifted to him as a prime suspect approximately two hours later and defendant was asked again if he had been advised of his rights and he answered in the affirmative, renewal of Miranda warnings was sufficient under the circumstances."[1]

---

[1] State v. Dixon, 107 Ariz. 415 (Ariz. 1971)

Homes

Home Defined

A person's home is the *most* protected area under the Fourth Amendment. Therefore, always tread lightly if you conduct a warrantless search or seizure inside a home.

Whether a particular place is deemed a "home" will depend upon whether the place provides a person with a reasonable expectation of privacy such that he would be justified in believing that he could retreat there, and be secure against government intrusion. In simple terms, where a person sleeps is usually his home.

GUIDELINES

Defining where a person lives is extremely important for many law enforcement activities, such as serving arrest warrants or whether a person has standing to contest a search.

Factors to consider:[1]

1. Length of stay;

2. Regular use (i.e. sleeps there on a regular basis);

3. Relationship to other occupants;

4. Storing possessions or receives mail there; and

5. Payment of rent.

CASE EXAMPLES

Hotel rooms have same protections as homes
The rule that a warrantless entry by police into a residence is presumptively unreasonable applies whether the entry is made to

---

[1] People v. White, 512 N.E.2d 677 (Ill. 1987)

search for evidence or to seize a person. It applies no less when the dwelling entered is a motel.[1]

A lawfully erected tent is equivalent to a home

"The thin walls of a tent are notice of its occupant's claim to privacy unless consent to enter be asked and given. One should be free to depart a campsite for the day's adventure without fear of his expectation of privacy being violated. Whether of short or longer term duration, one's occupation of a tent is entitled to equivalent protection from unreasonable government intrusion as that afforded to homes or hotel rooms."[2]

Subject had no reasonable expectation of privacy in illegal campsite

"Defendant had no authorization to camp within or otherwise occupy the public land. On at least four or five recent occasions he had been cited by officers for "illegal camping" and evicted from other campsites in the preserve. Thus, both the illegality, and defendant's awareness that he was illicitly occupying the premises without consent or permission, are undisputed. "Legitimation of expectations of privacy by law must have a source outside of the Fourth Amendment, either by reference to concepts of real or personal property law or to understandings that are recognized and permitted by society."[3]

Tent over vehicle at music festival was a home

Suspect went to music festival and pitched a 10'x30' tent-like structure over his SUV. Suspect was arrested for dealing drugs. Police conducted warrantless search on vehicle. Court held it was an illegal search inside "home." Tent was similar to a garage.[4]

Frequent visitor may have privacy inside home

A frequent visitor, with free reign of the house despite the fact that he did not stay overnight, might also have standing to contest an allegedly illegal entry of a third person's home.[5]

---

[1] People v. Williams, 45 Cal. 3d 1268 (Cal. 1988)
[2] People v. Hughston, 168 Cal. App. 4th 1062 (Cal. App. 1st Dist. 2008)
[3] People v. Nishi, 207 Cal. App. 4th 954 (Cal. App. 1st Dist. 2012)
[4] People v. Hughston, 168 Cal. App. 4th 1062 (Cal. App. 1st Dist. 2008)
[5] People v. Stewart, 113 Cal. App. 4th 242 (Cal. App. 1st Dist. 2003)

Hotel Rooms

Generally, hotel rooms receive full Fourth Amendment protections. You cannot enter a room without consent, recognized exception, or warrant (C.R.E.W.).

REPORT WRITING

A person doesn't have a reasonable expectation of privacy:

1. When the room has been abandoned; or

2. When the rental period has expired and money is owed on the room. Though money is an important factor, it's not the sole factor. You must look at the totality of circumstances and standard operating procedure of the hotel (does hotel have "grace period?"); or

3. When the occupants have been evicted by management.

CASE EXAMPLES

Police may assist in evicting occupants

"A defendant, justifiably evicted from his hotel room, has no reasonable expectation of privacy in the room under the Fourth Amendment and police may justifiably enter the room to assist the hotel manager in expelling the individuals in an orderly fashion."[1]

Hotel manager may not authorize search of occupant's room

Defendant was a suspect in an armed robbery. After police officers obtained information where defendant was staying, they went to the hotel and received permission from a hotel clerk to enter defendant's room, where they seized evidence without a warrant. Search held to be a violation of the Fourth Amendment.[2]

---

[1] United States v. Molsbarger, 551 F.3d 809 (8th Cir. N.D. 2009)
[2] Stoner v. California, 376 U.S. 483 (U.S. 1964)

Curtilage

The home is the most protected area of the Fourth Amendment. The space around the home, called curtilage, is also offered a high level of protection, though less than inside the home.

Whenever you run into a curtilage issue, the first question is whether or not the space is actually curtilage. If not, the area is considered an open-field and not protected by the Fourth Amendment.

If a space is deemed curtilage, the second question is how much protection is afforded to the space. Not all curtilage is created equal. The backyard, for example, is often protected more than the front yard. Police may knock on the front door, but it would be a violation to bring a drug detection canine.[1]

REPORT WRITING

Courts consider the following:[2]

1. The proximity of the area to the home itself;

2. Whether the area is included within a single enclosure, natural or artificial, surrounding the home;

3. The use of the area;

4. Steps taken by the resident to protect the area from observations by people passing by.

CASE EXAMPLES

Area around unoccupied trailer was not curtilage

A suspect had an uninhabited trailer on his property. Police looked around and saw a meth lab inside. Suspect argued the area

[1] Florida v. Jardines, 133 S. Ct. 1409 (U.S. 2013)
[2] United States v. Dunn, 480 U.S. 294 (U.S. 1987)

immediately surrounding the trailer was curtilage. Court held area around trailer was not curtilage.[1]

Private boat dock not curtilage

Police entered a private dock area, past a no trespassing sign, and looked around. The area was used by boaters who docked their boats there. Area was not curtilage or protected by the Fourth amendment.[2]

Observations from backyard unlawful

"While the Supreme Court has never required that law enforcement officers ... shield their eyes when passing by a home on public thoroughfares ... the officers still must observe the area being searched from a lawful vantage point. ... The officers in this case made the incriminating observations of the unattached garage while standing in a constitutionally protected area—the backyard."[3]

Observation from side yard of apartment lawful

"In sum, although the defendants could easily have shielded their activities from public view, they failed to take the simple and obvious steps necessary to do so. By exposing their illicit cocaine activities to the side yard —a place where they should have anticipated that other persons might have a right to be— defendants failed to exhibit a subjective expectation that they intended their dealings in the bedroom to be private. Hence, the police observations did not violate defendants' Fourth Amendment rights."[4]

Apartment lobby not curtilage

"[T]he only issue before us is whether tenants in a large, high-rise apartment building, the front door of which has an undependable lock that was inoperable on the day in question, have a reasonable expectation of privacy in the common areas of their building. Our answer is no. There was nothing to prevent anyone and everyone who wanted to do so from walking in the unlocked door and wandering freely about the premises."[5]

---

[1] Olson v. State, 166 Ga. App. 104 (Ga. Ct. App. 1983)
[2] United States v. Edmonds, 611 F.2d 1386 (5th Cir. Ga. 1980)
[3] Daughenbaugh v. City of Tiffin, 150 F.3d 594 (6th Cir. Ohio 1998)
[4] United States v. Fields, 113 F.3d 313 (2d Cir. Conn. 1997)
[5] United States v. Miravalles, 280 F.3d 1328 (11th Cir. Fla. 2002)

Trash Searches

It has been clearly established by the Supreme Court that a suspect has no reasonable expectation of privacy in trash that has been left out in order to be collected by the garbage company (i.e. trash has been "abandoned").

The key here is that the trash has been put out for collection. If the trash is within the curtilage, and the trash company doesn't pick-up trash from that location, it has not been abandoned...yet.

REPORT WRITING

1. Describe why the item was trash (in a trash can, in black lawn bag, etc.);

2. Describe where the item was abandoned. The further away from curtilage the better. Either way, articulate that the location where you picked up the trash was where the trash company collects it;

3. Describe when you picked up the trash (Tuesday @ 11pm) and how that time coincides with regular trash pickup (Wednesday morning). This is important because the defendant may try to argue that he intended to retrieve the trash before pickup; and

4. If the location is a business articulate how the general public could access the trash. If a business took affirmative steps to exclude the public (like locked fence), you'll need a warrant or have to wait until the trash company retrieves the trash.

CASE EXAMPLES

Seizing trash for 12 days straight not unlawful

Police seized an apartment dweller's trash for 12 days straight. Court held trash was abandoned.[1]

---

[1] Smith v. State, 510 P.2d 793 (Alaska 1973)

Open Fields

Open fields are those areas that don't receive any Fourth Amendment protections. Typically, these areas are literally "open fields," and there are no structures on them (like sheds). Sometimes police will commit a technical trespass in order to reach open fields and view evidence (e.g. marijuana grows). The Supreme Court has held that there is no constitutional violation because the open field itself is not "persons, houses, papers and effects" or an area where a person has a reasonable expectation of privacy.

GUIDELINES

If you want to inspect something that is on private property, you may do so without a warrant as long as the property is not within the curtilage of a home. Also, just because there is a physical structure on the open field doesn't mean it's curtilage (e.g. tool shed 300 feet away from home). You cannot enter any structure unless it was abandoned, even on open fields.

The "open fields" doctrine typically applies to any unoccupied or undeveloped area outside the curtilage of the property.

CASE EXAMPLES

The Fourth Amendment doesn't protect open fields

"[T]he special protection accorded by the Fourth Amendment to the people in their persons, houses, papers, and effects, is not extended to the open fields. The distinction between the latter and the house is as old as the common law."[1]

---

[1] Hester v. United States, 44 S. Ct. 445 (U.S. 1924)

Consent to Search and Co-Occupants

Law enforcement officers may seek consent to search a residence from co-occupants.[1] However, the situation changes when there is a present non-consenting co-occupant. If one occupant tells the cops to "Come on in" and another says "Get the hell out," well, police must stay out.[2]

What about areas under the exclusive control of the consenter? For example, the "cooperative" tenant says you can still search their bedroom? Or a shed they have exclusive control over in the backyard? There is no case that deals directly with this issue, but if the area is truly under the exclusive control of the consenting party, and you can articulate that the non-consenting party has no reasonable expectation of privacy in that area, I believe it would be reasonable to search just that area.

The best practice is to wait until the non-consenting occupant left the residence. In other words, if the non-consenting occupant goes to work, store, or is lawfully arrested, the remaining occupant can consent to search. However, do not search areas under the exclusive control of the non-consenting party. This could include file cabinets, "man-caves," and so forth.

Finally, if the consenting party has greater authority over the residence, then police may rely on the consent. For example, if a casual visitor or babysitter objected to police entry, it could be overruled by a homeowner. Still, police could not search personal property under the exclusive control of the visitor or babysitter.

REPORT WRITING

---

[1] United States v. Matlock, 415 U.S. 164 (U.S. 1974)
[2] Georgia v. Randolph, 126 S. Ct. 1515 (U.S. 2006)

How to articulate a lawfully removed non-consenting party:

1. Articulate why the non-consenting party was lawfully removed:

    o Arrested (domestic, warrant, etc.)

    o Lawfully evicted

    o Served with restraining order and required to leave

2. Describe how you re-approached the remaining occupant and received valid consent to enter and search (best practice is to provide a break in contact before regaining consent, two hours or more would be reasonable;

3. Describe how you didn't exceed the scope of the search. Remember, the remaining co-occupant may not have the authority to authorize entry into every area of the house (like roommate's bedroom or backpack;

Articulating greater authority:

If the consenting co-occupant has greater authority over the premises than the non-consenting party, police may enter and search common areas. For example, a homeowner would have greater authority than a babysitter, or a child. Articulate the following in your report:

1. Why the consenting co-occupant had greater authority;

2. Why the non-consenting co-occupant had less authority; and

3. You didn't search areas under the exclusive control of the non-consenting occupant.

CASE EXAMPLES

Consent of wife valid after non-consenting husband left residence

"The consent of one who possesses common authority over premises or effects" generally "is valid as against the absent, nonconsenting person with whom that authority is shared." (allowing admission of evidence found in a diaper bag in a bedroom closet following a search conducted pursuant to the consent of [the wife] with common authority over the bedroom).[1]

---

[1] United States v. Cordero-Rosario, 786 F.3d 64 (1st Cir. P.R. 2015)

Parental Consent to Search Child's Room

Typically, a parent can grant consent to search a child's room, particularly a minor child, even if the child objects to the search.

GUIDELINES

Minor children: Parents of minor children can almost always consent to search a child's belongings or living areas.

Adult children: Courts generally ask two questions:

1. Does the child pay rent (if so then it's likely a tenant/landlord relationship); or

2. Has the child taken steps to deny his parents access to the property or living area in question (if so then child may have a reasonable expectation of privacy).

CASE EXAMPLES

Parents may consent to search over a child's objection

"While there is no question minors are entitled to the protection of the Fourth Amendment, adults and minors are not necessarily entitled to the same degree of constitutional protection...To fulfill their duty of supervision, parents must be empowered to authorize police to search the family home, even over the objection of their minor children."[1]

---

[1] In re D.C., 188 Cal. App. 4th 978 (Cal. App. 1st Dist. 2010)

Mistaken Authority

If you're a prudent officer you normally ask for consent to search, even if you have P/C. Why? Because valid consent adds an extra layer of protection for your criminal case.

But sometimes you'll think you're dealing with an occupant who has the authority to consent, but later find out you were wrong. For example, the consent was received from a guest, not homeowner. Here, courts will look to see if your actions were reasonable.

GUIDELINES

Whenever police mistakenly receive consent from a person who has "apparent authority," courts will employ a three-part analysis to determine if your mistake was reasonable:[1]

1. Did you believe some untrue fact;

2. Was it objectively reasonable for you to believe that the fact was true under the circumstances; and

3. If it was true would the consent giver have had actual authority.

CASE EXAMPLES

Police may assume adult that answered door had authority

Police were trying to locate a robbery suspect and knocked on his door. A visitor answered and consented to their request to enter. "Police may assume, without further inquiry, that [an adult] person who answers the door in response to their knock has the authority to let them enter."[2]

---

[1] Ill. v. Rodriguez, 497 U.S. 177 (U.S. 1990)
[2] People v. Ledesma, 39 Cal. 4th 641 (Cal. 2006)

Warrantless Entry to Make Arrest

You cannot make a warrantless entry into a home to make an arrest without consent or exigency.[1] Even if the arrest was for a violent triple murder, you would have to articulate consent or exigency before entering.

GUIDELINES

Consent: You may enter if an occupant with apparent authority allows you to enter. Do not lie about your purpose ("I'm just here to talk"). If the suspect answers, tell him why you're there. Do not, under any circumstances, engage in "hot pursuit" if the suspect refuses entry and flees back into the house (unless you had legitimate exigency before knocking on door). The only exception is when the suspect actually crosses the threshold of the door and therefore enters a quasi-public place for arrest purposes (I still recommend warrant).

Hot pursuit: If you're chasing a suspect you're going to arrest, you may chase them into a protected area in order to make the arrest.[2] Alternatively, you could surround the home and call them out.

Fresh pursuit: If you're in fresh pursuit of a violent felony suspect you may make a warrantless entry to affect the arrest.

Prevent escape: You must articulate that if you don't make immediate entry the suspect will escape.[3]

Knock and announce rules apply (as always).

---

[1] Payton v. New York, 445 U.S. 573 (U.S. 1980)
[2] Stanton v. Sims, 134 S. Ct. 3 (U.S. 2013)
[3] Fletcher v. Town of Clinton, 196 F.3d 41 (1st Cir. Me. 1999)

Warrantless Arrest at Doorway (Threshold Doctrine)

Normally, you cannot enter a person's home to make a warrantless arrest. There are two exceptions, "exigency" and the "threshold doctrine." If a person is standing "in" their doorframe (i.e. threshold) you may physically take them into custody because the court views the threshold as quasi-public. Same logic applies to any area where the public has access, like porches. If the suspect runs you can chase them based upon hot pursuit.[1]

Tread lightly here because if the suspect successfully argues that he was a few inches inside his house, and not within the "threshold," it would be an unconstitutional entry and arrest.

GUIDELINES

If a suspect is standing within the threshold (i.e. doorframe), then you can make a warrantless arrest with probable cause.

Keep the following in mind:

1. The "threshold doctrine" is considered a quasi-public place for warrantless arrest purposes. However, the suspect literally has to be within the doorframe area;

2. Best practice, stay away from threshold arrests unless it's for a violent felony.

CASE EXAMPLES

Suspect standing in doorway was lawfully chased in hot pursuit
Standing in the doorway is a public place for arrest purposes.[2]

---

[1] People v. Hampton, 164 Cal. App. 3d 27 (Cal. App. 1st Dist. 1985)
[2] United States v. Santana, 427 U.S. 38 (U.S. 1976)

Warrantless Entry to Prevent Destruction of Evidence

Generally, you cannot make a warrantless entry into a home unless you have consent, recognized exception or a warrant (C.R.E.W.). One of the recognized exceptions is the warrantless entry to prevent the destruction of evidence.[1] Remember, that you cannot create the exigency. Simply knocking on the door does not count.

REPORT WRITING

1. Describe what evidence was inside the residence, and why recovering it was vital for your investigation;

2. Articulate how the evidence was being, or would be destroyed before you could obtain a search warrant. If necessary, describe how police didn't create the exigency;

3. Articulate how you complied with knock and announce;

4. Describe what you did once you entered the residence. I recommend you don't recover the evidence at this time. Instead, detain and seal the residence and seek a search warrant. This way you have judicial approval when you actually seize the evidence and can search for more evidence.

CASE EXAMPLES

Knocking on door and yelling police did not create the exigency

Officers smelled marijuana coming from apartment. After knocking on the door and saying "police" they heard suspects destroying evidence. Warrantless entry was lawful to preserve evidence.[2]

[1] Minnesota v. Olson, 495 U.S. 91 (U.S. 1990)
[2] Kentucky v. King, 563 U.S. 452 (U.S. 2011)

Detaining Residence in Anticipation of Search Warrant

If you're lawfully present inside a residence and discover evidence in plain view you may immediately seize the evidence. However, you would not have the authority to continue searching even if you had probable cause to do so. Instead, you would be required to "detain" the residence and seek a search warrant.

If appropriate, I recommend leaving the evidence how you found it and detaining (i.e. freezing) the residence until you get a warrant. There are a few advantages to this. First, the fact that evidence is positively inside the residence almost *guarantees* that a judge will authorize the warrant. Second, it shows the judge that you're not overzealous in your conduct and instead are seeking judicial approval. Finally, in the rare circumstance that your affidavit lacks probable cause the suspect would have almost no incentive to sue you since you didn't seize his property before judicial approval.

REPORT WRITING

If you detain a residence, articulate the following:

1. How you were lawfully inside the residence; Alternatively, articulate how you developed probable cause that evidence was inside the residence (C/I, investigation, witness, etc.);

2. Articulate why evidence would be destroyed or lost before warrant;

3. Professionally exclude all occupants and secure the residence;

4. Diligently apply for the warrant, unreasonable delay may lead to liability and suppression of evidence.[1]

---

[1] United States v. Song Ja Cha, 597 F.3d 995 (9th Cir. Guam 2010)

Detaining Containers in Anticipation of Search Warrant

If you develop probable cause that a container (package, luggage, etc.) contains evidence or contraband, you may seize it in order to seek a search warrant.[1] Remember, the length of the detention must be reasonable and the more "intimate" the container, the more courts will scrutinize the detention.

For example, detaining a woman's purse is more intimate than seizing an undelivered UPS parcel. A nine-hour detention on the purse may be struck down as excessive, where a two-day detention on the parcel may not. Either way diligently seek the warrant.

REPORT WRITING

If you detain a container, articulate the following:

1. Articulate how you developed probable cause that evidence was inside the container (C/I, investigation, witness, etc.);

2. If appropriate, articulate why evidence would be destroyed or lost before getting a warrant;

3. Describe when and where you seized the container and how you had lawful access;

4. Articulate in your warrant that you diligently sought judicial approval to seize the evidence inside the container.

---

[1] United States v. Hernandez, 314 F.3d 430 (9th Cir. Cal. 2002)

Warrantless Entry to Render Aid/Prevent Injury

Generally, you cannot make a warrantless entry into a home unless you have consent, recognized exception or a warrant (C.R.E.W.). One of the recognized exceptions is if you have an objective reasonable basis for believing that an occupant requires emergency assistance,[1] or an occupant is threatened with imminent injury.[2] Remember, the scope of your entry is limited and you must leave, if demanded, once the emergency is over.

REPORT WRITING

Articulate the following:

1. Describe facts and circumstances that made you believe that a person was inside the residence in need of immediate medical aid or was threatened with imminent injury;

2. Describe how you complied with knock and announce;

3. After entry, describe how you didn't exceed the scope of the reason for entry. Plain view applies;

4. You may make a warrantless arrest;

5. Once the emergency (or "exigency") is over you must leave unless the contact is converted into a consensual encounter.

---

[1] Michigan v. Fisher, 558 U.S. 45 (U.S. 2009)
[2] Brigham City v. Stuart, 547 U.S. 398 (U.S. 2006)

Warrantless Entry for Officer Safety

Generally, you cannot make a warrantless entry into a home unless you have consent, recognized exception or a warrant (C.R.E.W.). One of the recognized exceptions is when you have an objective reasonable basis for believing violence is imminent upon officers.

Courts have recognized two situations where this can occur. First, if you're making an arrest outside of a person's home (i.e. porch) and you have an objective reasonable basis to believe that someone inside the home is about to attack you, police may make entry and conduct a protective sweep.[1]

Second, if you're interviewing a suspect outside their home and they suddenly flee back into the home, you can follow them if you have an objective reasonable belief that they were going to get a weapon.[2]

Under either scenario, your authority to enter is extremely limited. Once the situation is safe, or your original belief is unfounded, you must leave unless converted into a consensual encounter.

REPORT WRITING

Protective sweep:

1. Describe any facts or circumstances that the suspect is violent or committed an act of violence;

2. Describe where the arrest took place (within curtilage) and how the suspect is associated with the residence;

3. Articulate why someone inside the house presented an imminent threat of violence;

---

[1] People v. Ormonde, 143 Cal. App. 4th 282 (Cal. App. 6th Dist. 2006)
[2] Ryburn v. Huff, 565 U.S. 469 (U.S. 2012)

4. Articulate that you entered to make a protective sweep after making an arrest. Plain view applies but I recommend you detain and secure the residence for a search warrant.

Flight into home to obtain a weapon:

1. Describe any facts or circumstances why the suspect is violent or may have committed an act of violence;

2. Describe where the interview took place (i.e front yard) and how the suspect is associated with the residence;

3. Describe any facts or circumstances why you objectively believed the suspect was fleeing back into the residence to gain access to a weapon;

4. Describe that you entered to prevent the suspect from gaining a weapon and attacking you. You cannot make a protective sweep unless you also believed someone else in the home was going to attack you. Plain view applies but you need a warrant to search for evidence.

CASE EXAMPLES

Judges should be cautious about second guessing officer safety

Officers in Burbank were investigating reports that a student was going to "shoot up" the school. They went to his house and spoke to his mother, who acted oddly and when asked about whether there were guns in the house quickly turned around and went into the house. Officers followed in case she was going to get a gun. She later sued for warrantless entry. "The Fourth Amendment permits an officer to enter a residence if the officer has a reasonable basis for concluding that there is an imminent threat of violence...Judges should be cautious about second-guessing a police officer's assessment, made on the scene, of the danger presented by a particular situation."[1]

---

[1] Ryburn v. Huff, 565 U.S. 469 (U.S. 2012)

Warrantless Entry to Investigate Child Abuse

If you have an objective reasonable basis to believe that a child needs protection or aid you may make a warrantless entry to investigate or render aid.[1]

REPORT WRITING

Articulate the following:

1. Describe why you thought a child was in danger or in need of protective custody;

2. If possible, seek consent to enter and investigate;

3. If denied consent articulate that a warrantless entry was made based on exigency because a child may be in need of aid or protection;[2]

4. Describe what you did in the home, and how you didn't exceed the scope of the entry. Once the exigency is over, or unfounded, you must leave unless the contact is converted into consensual encounter;

5. Plain view applies but I recommend you detain and secure the residence for a search warrant.

---

[1] People v. Brown, 6 Cal. App. 3d 619 (Cal. App. 4th Dist. 1970)
[2] People v. Payne, 75 Cal. App. 3d 601 (Cal. App. 1st Dist. 1977)

Warrantless Entry to Protect Property

If you have an objective reasonable basis to believe that a warrantless entry will help protect property from damage, such as theft or vandalism, you may enter the property in order to help secure it or to contact the owner.

REPORT WRITING

Articulate the following:

1. Describe why the property was likely to suffer damage:

    a. Commercial premises were found unlocked or unattended after hours[1]

    b. Smell of gas leak[2]

2. Describe what you did while inside the property:

    a. Looked for contact information

    b. Verified premises were unoccupied

    c. You cleared building and secured it

3. Plain view applies, but I recommend you detain and secure the premises and apply for a search warrant.

---

[1] People v. Parra, 30 Cal. App. 3d 729 (Cal. App. 4th Dist. 1973)
[2] People v. Stegman, 164 Cal. App. 3d 936 (Cal. App. 4th Dist. 1985)

Crime Scenes

Generally, you cannot make a warrantless entry into a home unless you have consent, recognized exception or a warrant (C.R.E.W.). There's a recognized exception to make a warrantless entry to render emergency aid to a shooting victim. However, it would be a violation to fully process the crime scene without first obtaining a search warrant.[1] There is no "crime scene exception" to the warrant requirement, even for a violent murder.

REPORT WRITING

Articulate the following:

1. Describe why police made the original warrantless entry;

2. Once the emergency is over and the call has transitioned to a criminal investigation, apply for a search warrant;

3. Describe how the scene was sealed and secured in anticipation for a search warrant.

CASE EXAMPLES

There is no "murder scene exception" to warrant requirement

The United States Supreme Court rejected the contention that there is a "murder scene exception" to the Warrant Clause of the Fourth Amendment. Police may make warrantless entries onto premises if they reasonably believe a person is in need of immediate aid and may make prompt warrantless searches of a homicide scene for possible other victims or a killer on the premises, but searching for evidence requires a warrant.[2]

---

[1] Mincey v. Arizona, 437 U.S. 385 (U.S. 1978)
[2] Flippo v. W. Va., 528 U.S. 11 (U.S. 1999)

Entry with Ruse

Generally, courts don't like "ruses." A ruse is where someone is tricked. However, it's okay to "lie" about your *identity*, but not your *purpose*. Example, as an undercover cop you couldn't sneak around a suspect's home during a drug buy, that would be a lie about purpose (i.e. there to buy drugs, not snoop around).

Guidelines

You cannot use a ruse in order to gain entry into a home unless you have a search warrant.

Additionally, it's inappropriate to use a ruse in order to gain entry into someone's home in order to arrest him. For example, if you planned to arrest a suspect (without arrest warrant) it would not be okay to conduct a knock and talk and lie to the subject that you wanted to come in, "to just talk." On the other hand, if your intention was to talk and during the conversation you developed P/C to arrest, you could make the warrantless arrest since you were lawfully inside the home. Do you see the subtle difference?

Alternatively, the majority of cases hold that you can use a ruse to get the subject to voluntarily exit the residence if you had P/C.[1] For example, you could tell a wanted suspect that his car was illegally parked and to move it even if not true.

Case Examples

Unlawful ruse by ATF agent who portrayed himself as state LEO

ATF tagged along with a CA DOJ agent to perform a licensing inspection. ATF was actually conducting a different investigation. Court held the entry was an unlawful ruse.[2]

---

[1] People v. Reyes, 83 Cal. App. 4th 7 (Cal. App. 4th Dist. 2000)
[2] United States v. Bosse, 898 F.2d 113 (9th Cir. Cal. 1990)

Suspect Exit with Ruse

Generally, you may be able to use a ruse to get a suspect to come out of their house if you have R/S or P/C.[1] Once the suspect is outside, you can arrest or detain him. "Outside" the home includes the front porch and anywhere the general public has lawful access. These areas usually include walkways to the front door and driveways.

GUIDELINES

If you try to convince a suspect to exit their home, but they instead try to close the door or retreat into the home, you cannot run after them.[2]

Be cautious whenever you use a ruse or trick. Keep in mind:

- If you have probable cause to arrest, it's best to come up with a ruse that includes identifying yourself as a police officer. For example, if true, you can tell the suspect that if they don't come outside and talk to you then you'll apply for a warrant which could result in the SWAT team serving an arrest warrant.

- If you have exigent circumstances to enter the home and arrest the suspect (e.g. hot/fresh pursuit) then it would also be lawful to surround and call out for officer safety purposes.

- Best practice, don't use ruses. They are heavily scrutinized.

CASE EXAMPLES

Unlawful ruse where plainclothes cop told citizen he just hit his car
Where subject came out to inspect damage on car, court held that ruse was unreasonable since even innocent people would leave their residence. Evidence from consent to search suppressed.[3]

---

[1] United States v. Rengifo, 858 F.2d 800 (1st Cir. R.I. 1988)
[2] People v. Hampton, 164 Cal. App. 3d 27 (Cal. App. 1st Dist. 1985)
[3] People v. Reyes, 83 Cal. App. 4th 7 (Cal. App. 4th Dist. 2000)

SWAT Surround & Callout

A barricaded suspect is one who poses a danger to himself or others and refuses to leave his residence. Often police will surround the house and attempt to convince the suspect to come out peacefully. Surrounding a home is a seizure under the Fourth Amendment and must be justified by exigency (usually not an issue).

If the subject is suicidal the recognized exception is the "community caretaking doctrine." Often there's no crime committed by the subject (attempting suicide is not a crime) and police are trying to take the suspect into custody for a mental evaluation.

REPORT WRITING

Articulate the following:

1. Why were police called to the residence;

2. What factors made immediate entry dangerous to responding officers or other citizens;

3. If you intend to search for evidence after the standoff, you need a warrant or consent.

CASE EXAMPLES

No warrant needed during a surround and callout

During an armed standoff, once exigent circumstances justify the warrantless seizure of the suspect in his home, and so long as the police are actively engaged in completing his arrest, the police need not obtain an arrest warrant before taking the suspect into full physical custody.[1]

---

[1] Fisher v. City of San Jose, 558 F.3d 1069 (9th Cir. Cal. 2009)

Protective Sweeps

If you make a lawful arrest inside a home, you're allowed to conduct a protective sweep.[1] There are three zones, or areas, you may search depending on the circumstances.

Guidelines

Zone 1: This is the area within the lunge distance of the arrestee. You can search this area, and open any container, for evidence, weapons or means of escape.

Zone 2: You can look into areas inside the room where the arrest took place for subjects who may attack you. You can only look in people-sized places and cannot look for evidence. Plain view applies.

Zone 3: If you have reasonable suspicion that there are dangerous subjects somewhere else in the residence, you may look in people-sized places where they could be hiding. Plain view applies.

Case Example

Severity of crime committed can help justify protective sweep
"(T)he type of criminal conduct underlying the arrest or search is significant in determining if a protective sweep is justified."[2] Generalized safety concerns are not enough.[3]

Protective sweep of adjoining areas must be justified
Protective sweeps of the areas of the home beyond the immediate area (i.e., any adjoining rooms) of the arrest will not be upheld absent an articulable reason for believing someone in the home is present who constitutes a potential danger to the officers.[4]

---

[1] Maryland v. Buie, 494 U.S. 325 (U.S. 1990)
[2] People v. Ledesma, 106 Cal. App. 4th 857 (Cal. App. 1st Dist. 2003)
[3] People v. Werner, 207 Cal. App. 4th 1195 (Cal. App. 6th Dist. 2012)
[4] United States v. Furrow, 229 F.3d 805 (9th Cir. Idaho 2000)

Businesses

Customer Business Records

Generally, a customer has no reasonable expectation of privacy in information kept by a third party. Therefore, you may request access to business records. However, if access is denied then a court order, subpoena, or search warrant is required. You cannot demand a business consensually supply their records.

GUIDELINES

Phone Company Records: A search does not occur when police obtain the numbers dialed from a phone;[1]

Bank Records: The use of bank records does not constitute a search under the Fourth Amendment;[2]

Business Records: An individual does not have a privacy interest in the records of the business he patronizes.[3]

CASE EXAMPLES

Customer has no reasonable expectation of privacy in banking records

"The Fourth Amendment protects against intrusions into an individual's zone of privacy. In general, a depositor has no reasonable expectation of privacy in bank records, such as checks, deposit slips, and financial statements maintained by the bank. Where an individual's Fourth Amendment rights are not implicated, obtaining the documents does not violate his or her rights, even if the documents lead to indictment."[4]

---

[1] Smith v. Md., 442 U.S. 735 (U.S. 1979)
[2] United States v. Miller, 425 U.S. 435 (U.S. 1976)
[3] In re Grand Jury Subpoenas Duces Tecum., 78 F.3d 1307 (8th Cir. Ark. 1996)
[4] Marsoner v. United States (In re Grand Jury Proceedings), 40 F.3d 959 (9th Cir. Ariz. 1994)

Warrantless Arrest Inside Business

Generally, you may enter "public areas" of a business to make an arrest. However, you don't have an automatic right, even when you possess an arrest warrant, to enter business offices and other areas where there is a reasonable and legitimate expectation of privacy.[1] These areas are typically areas where the public doesn't have access.

GUIDELINES

You may make the arrest if the suspect is in a public area of the business;

If the suspect is in an area where the general public does not have access, you would need consent (from anyone with apparent authority), exigency, or a search warrant.

CASE EXAMPLES

Entry into closed portion of business unlawful

Officers entered a casino and then entered a bingo hall that was presently closed to the public. Officers saw evidence of illegal gambling. Since bingo hall was not presently accessible to the public, the court suppressed the evidence.[2]

---

[1] Steagald v. United States, 451 U.S. 204 (U.S. 1981)
[2] State v. Foreman, 662 N.E.2d 929 (Ind. 1996)

Closely Regulated Businesses

In general, businesses enjoy Fourth Amendment protections. One notable exception is when you conduct warrantless inspections of "closely regulated" businesses. These include bars, gun stores, and junk yards.

GUIDELINES

You should first seek consent before you inspect a closely regulated business. If you are denied entry you can nevertheless make a warrantless entry if your government's regulatory scheme (codes, ordinances, statutes) includes no-notice inspections so that the business is on notice. Remember, the warrantless search must be authorized by law, otherwise police must get a warrant.[1]

CASE EXAMPLES

Owners of closely regulated businesses are on notice for warrantless searches

"Certain industries have such a history of government oversight that no reasonable expectation of privacy could exist for a proprietor over the stock of such an enterprise. Liquor ... and firearms ... are industries of this type; when an entrepreneur embarks upon such a business, he has voluntarily chosen to subject himself to a full arsenal of governmental regulation."[2]

---

[1] Colonnade Catering Corp. v. United States, 90 S. Ct. 774 (U.S. 1970)
[2] Marshall v. Barlow's, Inc., 98 S. Ct. 1816 (U.S. 1978)

Government Workplace Searches

The Fourth Amendment applies to all government searches and seizures, including government workplace searches and drug tests.[1] However, the Supreme Court has significantly lowered the bar for these searches and they are generally upheld if conducted for a legitimate purpose and carried out in a reasonable manner. A government supervisor may search an employee's desk, filing cabinets, or other areas without a warrant or probable cause so long as the search is reasonable at its inception and reasonable in scope. As the Supreme Court noted:

> In our view, requiring an employer to obtain a warrant whenever the employer wished to enter an employee's office, desk, or file cabinets for a work-related purpose would seriously disrupt the routine conduct of business and would be unduly burdensome.[2]

REPORT WRITING

Articulate the following:

1. Prior notice to the employee that limits their reasonable expectation of privacy;

2. Common practices of the employer;

3. Openness and accessibility of the area or item in question;

4. Whether the position of the employee requires a special trust and confidence (e.g. police and those with security clearances); and

5. Whether the employee waived their rights (helps, not required).

---

[1] City of Ontario v. Quon, 560 U.S. 746 (U.S. 2010)
[2] O'Connor v. Ortega, 107 S. Ct. 1492 (U.S. 1987)

Fire, Health and Safety Searches

Generally, businesses enjoy Fourth Amendment protections. One notable exception is "fire, health and safety" inspections.

REPORT WRITING

1. Seek consent before you conduct a fire, health or safety inspection of an area closed off to the public.

2. If you are denied entry, seek an administrative warrant. These warrants don't require probable cause. Instead, they require a regulatory framework (food inspection, fire system safety check, etc.) and evidence that the inspector has been denied entry.

3. If applicable, review "closely regulated businesses" in this book.

CASE EXAMPLES

OSHA inspections require a warrant without consent

OSHA attempted to make a safety inspection on a plumbing business. The owner denied OSHA entry, saying that they needed to get a warrant first. The Court held that it was not overly burdensome for OSHA to get a warrant if consent was denied.[1]

---

[1] Marshall v. Barlow's, Inc., 436 U.S. 307 (U.S. 1978)

Vehicles

Randomly Running License Plates

A driver has no Fourth Amendment protection in their license plate. Officers are permitted to run license plates randomly, without any suspicion. Any information gained from the plate query can be used as evidence.

Guidelines

You can randomly query license plates through state and federal databases.

Case Examples

Stolen plates were in plain view

The court found that the initial detention of defendant was justified under Terry. The vehicle defendant was driving was a civilian vehicle with a military plate and thus, the officers were justified in believing that they had encountered possible criminal behavior in that either the car or the military plate was stolen. Because the military plate was in plain view on the outside of the car, it was subject to seizure. Further, the vehicle registration was given voluntarily to the military policeman in response to a request for identification and thus, was not seized as the result of any search. Additionally, there was probable cause for the initial search of the vehicle for evidence pertaining to its theft because there was probable cause to believe the car and the military plate were stolen. Likewise, the second search, which was an inventory search, was made pursuant to standard police practice. [1]

---

[1] United States v. Matthews, 615 F.2d 1279 (10th Cir. Colo. 1980)

Community Caretaking Stops

You may make a traffic stop on a vehicle if you believe any of the occupant's safety or welfare is at risk.[1] If you determine that the occupant does not need assistance, you must terminate the stop or transition the stop into a consensual encounter. Otherwise, you would need to articulate reasonable suspicion (e.g. DUI) or other criminal involvement.

Stranded motorists fall under this rule. It's not illegal for a vehicle to break down. So, you cannot demand ID, or otherwise involuntarily detain stranded motorists unless you can articulate they are involved in criminal activity.

REPORT WRITING

If you make a community caretaking stop, articulate the following:[2]

1. The nature and level of the distress exhibited by the individual;

2. The location of the individual (e.g. stranded on side of road);

3. Whether or not the individual was alone and/or had access to assistance independent of that offered by the officer;

4. To what extent the individual—if not assisted—presented a danger to himself or others; and

5. Articulate that the purpose of the search was to render aid.

---

[1] People v. Madrid, 168 Cal. App. 4th 1050 (Cal. App. 1st Dist. 2008)
[2] Wright v. State, 7 S.W.3d 148 (Tex. Crim. App. 1999)

Reasonable Suspicion Stops

You can stop a vehicle if you have individualized reasonable suspicion that that any occupant may be involved in criminal activity. Probable cause is not required.

REPORT WRITING

If you make a reasonable suspicion stop on a vehicle, articulate the following:

1. Any observations that an occupant may be involved in criminal activity; or

2. Any facts or circumstances that would lead a reasonable officer to believe that the occupants are about to be involved in criminal activity; and

3. If necessary, describe your training and experience. Remember, as a trained police officer you may interpret apparently innocent behavior as indicating criminal conduct.

4. The key to any R/S stop is to articulate, articulate, articulate.

CASE EXAMPLES

Stop of possible stolen truck, even with different plates, reasonable

Observation of a truck that matched the description of one that had just been stolen in a carjacking, but with a different license plate that appeared to be recently attached, and with two occupants who generally matched the suspects' description, constituted the necessary reasonable suspicion to justify the defendant's detention.[1]

---

[1] United States v. Hartz, 458 F.3d 1011 (9th Cir. Wash. 2006)

DUI Checkpoints

The Supreme Court has upheld DUI checkpoints because the state's interest in preventing accidents caused by drunk drivers is outweighed by the minimal intrusion upon driver's who are temporarily stopped.[1]

GUIDELINES

Keep these factors in mind:

1. The checkpoint should be conducted in a systematic manner;

2. Police cannot indiscriminately stop drivers unless there's individualized suspicion;

3. The checkpoint itself must be "minimally intrusive;"

4. There's no set time limit for how long you can stop drivers, but a good rule of thumb is the average length of a traffic signal (20-120 seconds);

5. Clear the traffic queue if excessive delays develop; and

6. Police should limit their driver interview to quickly confirming or dispelling whether or not the driver is DUI.

Note: Don't get sucked-in by drivers who record you at checkpoints. Often these drivers only roll their window down a few inches and refuse to answer all of your questions. If you think they're sober and just playing games, let them go.

CASE EXAMPLE

Evasive driving away from roadblock

"Evasive behavior in response to a roadblock" may contribute to reasonable suspicion that the driver is possibly DUI."[2]

---

[1] Mich. Dep't of State Police v. Sitz, 496 U.S. 444 (U.S. 1990)
[2] United States v. Smith, 396 F.3d 579 (4th Cir. N.C. 2005)

License & Registration Checkpoints

The Supreme Court has suggested that a DUI style checkpoint to verify driver's licenses and vehicle registrations would be permissible.[1]

> A state is not precluded from developing methods for spot checks that involve less intrusion or that do not involve the unconstrained exercise of discretion. Persons in automobiles on public roadways may not for that reason alone have their travel and privacy interfered with at the unbridled discretion of police officers.

However, it is suggested that you run this proposed practice by legal counsel first.

GUIDELINES

Keep two factors in mind:[2]

1. The checkpoint should be conducted in a systematic manner. Police cannot indiscriminately stop drivers unless there's individualized suspicion; and

2. The checkpoint itself must be "minimally intrusive." If traffic gets excessively delayed police should clear the traffic queue and start over. Also, police should limit their driver interview to quickly confirming or dispelling whether or not the driver is licensed.

• See DUI Checkpoints for more information.

---

[1] Delaware v. Prouse, 440 U.S. 648 (U.S. 1979)
[2] Mich. Dep't of State Police v. Sitz, 496 U.S. 444 (U.S. 1990)

Information-Gathering Checkpoints

Police are permitted to setup checkpoints in order to gather information concerning a serious crime that has been recently committed. An example would be asking motorists if they witnessed a fatal accident that occurred a week ago.

Guidelines

Factors the Court considered:

1. The Court stated that "special police concerns" will sometimes justify a highway stop without individualized suspicion;

2. The checkpoint sought information, not criminal conduct;

3. The checkpoint was setup one week after the incident;

4. Finally, the checkpoint was established in the area of the accident and therefore more likely to run across witnesses.

If criminal activity is observed in plain view, investigate.

Case Examples

Information checkpoint upheld after fatal hit-and-run

About 1 week after a hit-and-run accident killed a bicyclist, local police set up a checkpoint, to obtain information from motorists about the accident. Officers asked motorists whether they had seen anything and handed out flyers. As one driver approached, his van swerved, nearly hitting an officer. The officer smelled alcohol, administered a sobriety test and then arrested the driver. The Supreme Court upheld the checkpoint as reasonable. [1]

---

[1] Illinois v. Lidster, 540 U.S. 419 (U.S. 2004)

Drug Checkpoints

The Supreme Court has never approved a checkpoint program whose primary purpose was to detect evidence of ordinary criminal wrong doing (such as drug possession).

Guidelines

When police establish a checkpoint, they are temporarily seizing citizens. Therefore, the seizure must be based on individualized reasonable suspicion or the checkpoint must be conducted in a reasonable manner as outlined in Sitz (see DUI checkpoints).

Case Examples

Narcotics checkpoint held unlawful

The purpose of the narcotics checkpoints was to advance "the general interest in crime control," We decline to suspend the usual requirement of individualized suspicion where the police seek to employ a checkpoint primarily for the ordinary enterprise of investigating crimes. [1]

Imminent terrorist attack checkpoint would be lawful

Of course, there are circumstances that may justify a law enforcement checkpoint where the primary purpose would otherwise, but for some emergency, relate to ordinary crime control. For example, as the Court of Appeals noted, the Fourth Amendment would almost certainly permit an appropriately tailored roadblock set up to thwart an imminent terrorist attack or to catch a dangerous criminal who is likely to flee by way of a particular route. [2]

---

[1] City of Indianapolis v. Edmond, 531 U.S. 32 (U.S. 2000)
[2] Id.

Management Considerations for all Checkpoints

Police supervisors should address these factors in any checkpoint operations plan.[1]

Report Writing

1. The decision to establish a sobriety checkpoint, the selection of the site, and the procedures for the operation of the checkpoint, are made and established by supervisory law enforcement personnel;

2. Motorists are stopped according to a neutral formula, such as every third, fifth or tenth driver;[2]

3. Adequate safety precautions are taken, such as proper lighting, warning signs, and signals, and clearly identifiable official vehicles and personnel;

4. The location of the checkpoint was determined by a policy-making official, and was reasonable; i.e., on a road having a high incidence of alcohol-related accidents or arrests;

5. The time the checkpoint was conducted and its duration reflect "good judgment" on the part of law enforcement officials;

6. The checkpoint exhibits indicia of its official nature (to reassure the public of the authorized nature of the stop);

7. The average length and nature of the detention is minimized.

8. The checkpoint is preceded by publicity.[3]

---

[1] Ingersoll v. Palmer, 43 Cal. 3d 1321 (Cal. 1987)
[2] Mich. Dep't of State Police v. Sitz, 496 U.S. 444 (U.S. 1990)
[3] Robert C. Phillips, California Search And Seizure Guide

Stops to Verify Temporary Registration

You cannot stop a vehicle solely to verify that a temporary registration is valid and/or not fraudulent. Even if you have a "hunch" that the registration is fake, you need to be able to articulate individualized articulable suspicion that a particular vehicle may have fraudulent registration. It is irrelevant that based on your "training and experience" temporary permits are often forged.[1]

REPORT WRITING

Articulate that a particular temp tag may be fraudulent:

1. Temp tag appeared altered;

2. Incorrect size or format;

3. No temp tag visible;

4. History that driver has altered tags previously;

5. Other articulable reasons.

CASE EXAMPLES

Stop to verify temp tag held unlawful

In November, a deputy stopped a vehicle with expired license plates. The deputy confirmed through dispatch that the registration had expired two months earlier but the renewal was "in process." The deputy also observed that a temporary operating permit with the number "11" (for November) had been taped to the window. Court held stop unlawful and evidence suppressed.[2]

---

[1] People v. Hernandez, 45 Cal. 4th 295 (Cal. 2008)
[2] People v. Brendlin, 45 Cal. 4th 262 (Cal. 2008)

Pretext Stops

You may only stop a vehicle if you have reasonable suspicion or probable cause that an offense has been, or will be, committed. It doesn't matter what you subjectively thought about the driver or passengers. What matters is objective reasonableness. Additionally, it would be unlawful to *unreasonably extend* the stop while you pursued a hunch. If you develop reasonable suspicion that the occupants are involved in criminal activity, then you may diligently pursue a means of investigation that will confirm or dispel those suspicions.

REPORT WRITING

Articulate the following:

1. Courts will not consider your subjective mindset;

2. Focus on the lawful reason for the stop;

3. If you develop additional reasonable suspicion or probable cause for other crimes, articulate that in your report and describe how you transitioned the stop from the investigation of a traffic offence to other criminal activity, like drugs. If possible, gain consent for any subsequent searches.

CASE EXAMPLES

Stop by undercover narcotics officers for minor violation upheld

D.C. detectives in an unmarked vehicle had a hunch that two suspects were dealing narcotics. The only violation they observed was failure to use a turn signal. Their stop violated a policy that unmarked vehicles could only make stops for serious crimes. Drugs were observed in plain view. Court held that the subjective mindset of the officers was irreverent as long as the initial stop was legal.[1]

---

[1] Whren v. United States, 517 U.S. 806 (U.S. 1996)

'Occupant' Defined

An occupant is any person inside the vehicle when the stop is made, or any person who was inside the vehicle moments before the stop.[1] Why is this important? Because if a person qualifies as an occupant of a vehicle, and is near that vehicle when they are arrested, you can conduct a warrantless search on that vehicle for evidence incident to arrest.

REPORT WRITING

Articulate the following:

1. Describe whether you saw the suspect inside the vehicle before you were able to detain them;

2. Describe where the suspect was found relative to the vehicle;

3. If arrested, indicate whether the suspect had the keys to the vehicle.

CASE EXAMPLES

Driver, who exited vehicle before police pulled up, was a "recent occupant"

An officer observed the defendant make an unsafe left hand turn, which caused oncoming traffic to slam on their brakes. By the time the officer caught up to the vehicle the driver had exited and was walking away. The driver was later arrested for no license and the search incident to arrest of vehicle was lawful.[2] Note, the driver would still need to be "unrestrained" and near the vehicle during the search. This practice is becoming very rare for officer safety reasons and therefore this exception is rarely used.

---

[1] Thornton v. United States, 541 U.S. 615 (U.S. 2004)
[2] United States v. Mapp, 476 F.3d 1012 (D.C. Cir. 2007)

Duration of Traffic Stop

Traffic stops can last no longer than reasonably necessary to handle the reason for the stop. It makes sense that a DUI stop will take longer than an equipment violation. Also, a traffic stop will last longer if you're writing a ticket than just giving a verbal warning. As long as you're diligently working on the stop you should be fine. Once the purpose of the stop is over, the driver must be *allowed* to leave.[1]

You may ask miscellaneous questions without additional reasonable suspicion, but unrelated inquires must not measurably extend the stop. "A seizure that is justified solely by the interest in issuing a warning ticket to the driver can become unlawful if it is prolonged beyond the time reasonably required to complete that mission."[2]

REPORT WRITING

Articulate the following:

1. Describe the reason for the original stop;

2. Describe how you diligently pursued the reason for the original stop (running suspects, writing ticket, etc.), but also articulate facts and circumstances that developed into reasonable suspicion or probable cause for other criminal activity. Write in your report the approximate time you transitioned the stop into an investigation for other criminal activity;

3. Most courts recognize that a routine traffic stop will take about 10-15 minutes;

4. If you can't develop reasonable suspicion before the stop is over, try to transition the stop into a consensual encounter.

---

[1] United States v. Salzano, 1998 U.S. App. LEXIS 17140 (10th Cir. Kan. 1998)
[2] Illinois v. Caballes, 125 S. Ct. 834 (U.S. 2005)

Incidental Questioning

The Supreme Court stated, "An officer's inquiries into matters unrelated to the justification for the traffic stop...do not convert the encounter into something other than a lawful seizure, so long as those inquires do not measurably extend the duration of the stop."[1]

Officers can ask various questions, such as where the driver is coming from, going to, where they work, etc. If you develop additional reasonable suspicion, then articulate those facts and circumstances in your report.

REPORT WRITING

Articulate how your unrelated inquires did not <u>measurably extend</u> the traffic stop.

CASE EXAMPLES

Unrelated inquires cannot measurably extend stop

"An officer's inquiries into matters unrelated to the justification for the traffic stop...do not convert the encounter into something other than a lawful seizure, so long as those inquiries do not measurably extend the duration of the stop."[2]

An officer may further detain occupant with additional reasonable suspicion

"[T]he officer may detain the driver for questioning unrelated to the initial stop if he has an objectively reasonable and articulable suspicion illegal activity has occurred or is occurring. ... A variety of factors may contribute to the formation of an objectively reasonable suspicion of illegal activity."[3]

---

[1] Arizona v. Johnson, 555 U.S. 323 (U.S. 2009)
[2] Id.
[3] United States v. Hunnicutt, 135 F.3d 1345 (10th Cir. Okla. 1998)

Consent to Search Vehicle

There is no Fourth Amendment violation if you seek consent to search a vehicle from a lawfully stopped driver.[1] Whether consent was voluntarily given will be judged by the totality of the circumstances. If consent to search is received, it will not be considered an unreasonable extension of the traffic stop.

REPORT WRITING

Articulate the following:

1. Consent should be obtained before the traffic stop is concluded, otherwise the consent may be tainted by an unlawful detention;

2. Describe how the consent was voluntarily given:

    a. Driver's age

    b. Experience/education

    c. Cooperative environment

    d. Driver was told of the right to refuse (not required)

    e. Lack of coercive police conduct, etc.

3. Describe how you did not exceed any limitations on scope of search, whether expressed or implied.[2]

4. Finally, describe how the suspect was able to revoke consent or alter scope at any time. Suspect should have constant access to an officer in order to communicate these conditions.

[1] Schneckloth v. Bustamonte, 412 U.S. 218 (U.S. 1973)
[2] Florida v. Jimeno, 500 U.S. 248 (U.S. 1991)

K9 Sniff Around Vehicle

Generally, there's no Fourth Amendment protection of the air around a vehicle.[1] Therefore, you can run a drug detection canine around a vehicle during a traffic stop or when the vehicle is left in a place that you're lawfully allowed to be, like a parking lot. If the canine alerts that would give you probable cause to either search it under the mobile conveyance exception or to apply for a warrant.

Keep in mind two important restrictions. First, do not intentionally command the canine to touch, climb or jump onto a vehicle as this would violate U.S. v. Jones.[2] Second, the canine sniff cannot extend the traffic stop unless you had reasonable suspicion for a drug offense. It's fine if one officer ran the canine while another handled the traffic stop.

Rᴇᴘᴏʀᴛ Wʀɪᴛɪɴɢ

Articulate the following:

1. If you don't have reasonable suspicion, articulate that the canine sniff did not unreasonably extend the stop;[3]

2. If you have reasonable suspicion, you may extend the traffic stop for a reasonable amount of time until the canine arrives. Note, if the canine takes an unreasonable amount of time to arrive the stop may turn into a de facto arrest requiring probable cause.

Cᴀsᴇ Exᴀᴍᴘʟᴇs

Use of K9 during a stop is reasonable

No violation where one officer wrote ticket while another ran drug dog.[4]

---

[1] United States v. Place, 462 U.S. 696 (U.S. 1983)
[2] United States v. Jones, 565 U.S. 400 (U.S. 2012)
[3] Illinois v. Caballes, 543 U.S. 405 (U.S. 2005)
[4] United States v. Hernandez-Mendoza, 600 F.3d 971 (8th Cir. S.D. 2010)

Reliability of K9's

According to the Supreme Court, there is no rigid checklist for determining the reliability of a drug detection canine. Courts must apply the totality of the circumstances test.

GUIDELINES

1. The mere fact that a canine alerted and no drugs were found doesn't automatically mean the dog is unreliable because of the canine's ability to detect residue odors.

2. The initial certification, along with the weekly training records should be sufficient to establish reliability.

CASE EXAMPLES

Courts look at the totality of the dog's training

Evidence of a dog's satisfactory performance in a narcotics certification or training program can itself provide sufficient reason to trust his alert. If a bona fide organization has certified a dog after testing his reliability in a controlled setting, a court can presume (subject to any conflicting evidence offered) that the dog's alert provides probable cause to search. The same is true, even in the absence of formal certification, if the dog has recently and successfully completed a training program that evaluated his proficiency in locating drugs. A defendant, however, must have an opportunity to challenge such evidence of a dog's reliability, whether by cross-examining the testifying officer or by introducing his own fact or expert witnesses.[1]

---

[1] Florida v. Harris, 133 S. Ct. 1050 (U.S. 2013)

Search for Driver's License and Vehicle Paperwork

If a driver, upon your request, "fails to produce" the necessary documentation necessary to issue a citation, you may have the right to conduct a limited search for his driver's license or vehicle registration.

> It is constitutionally proper for an officer to conduct a limited warrant-less search of a vehicle for the purpose of locating registration and other related identifying documentation.[1]

You may be allowed to search any area in the vehicle where the documents or identification may reasonably be expected to be found, but rarely includes the trunk.

Report Writing

1. Describe what the driver told you when you asked for their driver's license and vehicle paperwork. It will be easier to justify making a warrantless search if the driver refused to provide their paperwork, versus stating that they didn't have it;

2. If you believe the driver was lying or being deceitful about having identification or paperwork, articulate why;

3. Finally, describe how the search was confined only to areas or containers where the documents could reasonably be expected to be found.

---

[1] In re Arturo D., 27 Cal. 4th 60 (Cal. 2002)

Detention of Passengers

The Supreme Court has stated that passengers are seized under the Fourth Amendment during traffic stops. This also means that they can challenge the constitutionality of the stop if they are later charged with a crime.[1]

You're allowed to order passengers out of a vehicle,[2] or alternatively, order them to stay in the vehicle if they demand to leave, even if they haven't committed any offense.[3] The courts acknowledge the risks associated with traffic stops and the intrusion upon controlling passengers is minimal.

REPORT WRITING

If you order a passenger out of the vehicle, articulate why you did so:

- For any officer safety reason;
- To conduct separate interviews;
- To search the vehicle.

If a passenger is prevented from leaving, articulate why:

- For any officer safety reason;
- Vehicle is stopped on highway and it would be illegal for passenger to disembark at that location;
- You have reasonable suspicion of criminal activity and passenger may be involved or implicated after a search for evidence.

---

[1] Brendlin v. California, 551 U.S. 249 (U.S. 2007)
[2] Md. v. Wilson, 519 U.S. 408 (U.S. 1997)
[3] Arizona v. Johnson, 555 U.S. 323 (U.S. 2009)

Identifying Passengers

There is never a constitutional violation if you simply *request* a passenger identify themselves.[1] However, it is unclear whether you can *demand* identification when you have no reasonable suspicion passengers were involved in criminal activity.

One court held that the additional request for identification was not an "additional seizure" under the Fourth Amendment.[2] Additionally, the majority of courts acknowledge the officer safety risks inherent in traffic stops.[3] Therefore, it is plausible that if you demand identification from a passenger, it may be held lawful as long as it does not unreasonably prolong the traffic stop.

My advice is to not push the issue unless you have a very legitimate reason. Hopefully, you would have developed at least reasonable suspicion and if your state requires that suspects identify themselves during an R/S stop, you can make an arrest if the passenger refuses to identify themselves.[4] Also, passengers are not required to provide an actual government identification. At the very least they only have to provide a name and date of birth.

REPORT WRITING

If you demand identification from a passenger articulate the following:

1. Articulate how you requested the passenger to identify himself and he refused;

2. Describe why you needed to identify the passenger, even if you had no reasonable suspicion:

    a. Passenger made furtive movements;

---

[1] People v. Vibanco, 151 Cal. App. 4th 1 (Cal. App. 6th Dist. 2007)
[2] Id.
[3] Pa. v. Mimms, 434 U.S. 106 (U.S. 1977)
[4] Hiibel v. Sixth Judicial Dist. Court, 542 U.S. 177 (U.S. 2004)

> b. Other occupants are known gang members;
>
> c. You believe the passenger was wanted;
>
> d. Any other officer safety motive;

3. Articulate that you only ordered them to identify themselves, not necessarily provide a government identification;

4. Finally, articulate that since he had already been lawfully seized (because of the traffic stop), ordering him to identify himself was minimally intrusive;

5. If the passenger still refuses to identify themselves do not make an arrest unless you are sure they are engaged in criminal activity, like fugitive from justice. In many situations, the passenger may be acting more like a Constitutionalist or Sovereign Citizen and in these situations, I would not make arrest.

CASE EXAMPLES

Officers may ask passenger for identification

"After a lawful traffic stop, an officer may complete routine tasks, which may include asking a passenger for identification and running a computer check if the passenger consents to the request for identification."[1]

Asking for identification doesn't implicate the Fourth Amendment

Asking passenger for identification while he was lawfully detained did not implicate the Fourth Amendment because the police did not need to have reasonable suspicion in order to ask questions or request identification.[2]

Even if occupant wasn't going to drive, asking for ID lawful

"The fact that defendant indicated she didn't want to drive didn't alter the officer's ability to lawfully request identification during a lawful traffic stop. Officer Masucci then saw the scale in plain view as defendant opened her purse."[3]

---

[1] United States v. Cloud, 594 F.3d 1042 (8th Cir. Minn. 2010)

[2] People v. Vibanco, 151 Cal. App. 4th 1 (Cal. App. 6th Dist. 2007)

[3] People v. Lopez, 2008 Cal. App. Unpub. LEXIS 5586 (Cal. App. 2d Dist. July 10, 2008)

Ordering Occupants Out of Vehicle

Generally, you may order the driver[1] or passenger[2] out of a lawfully stopped vehicle for the duration of the traffic stop. It is unclear how much force, if any, you could use in order to make the passenger comply with your order. Instead, before using any force arrest the suspect for obstruction. The key here is to articulate all of the pertinent facts and circumstances and be reasonable in your actions.

Guidelines

You may order any occupant out of a motor vehicle for any legitimate reason. These reasons include:

1. Safety concerns
2. Investigative reasoning
3. Interviews
4. Vehicle searches

Case Examples

Officer can order occupant out of vehicle for any legitimate reason

"[O]nce a motor vehicle has been lawfully detained for a traffic violation, the police officers may order the driver to get out of the vehicle without violating the Fourth Amendment's proscription of unreasonable searches and seizures. An officer making a traffic stop may order passengers to get out of the car pending completion of the stop as well."[3]

---

[1] Pa. v. Mimms, 434 U.S. 106 (U.S. 1977)
[2] Md. v. Wilson, 519 U.S. 408 (U.S. 1997)
[3] Arizona v. Johnson, 129 S. Ct. 781 (U.S. 2009)

Patdown of Occupants

If you can reasonably articulate that any occupant is armed and dangerous, you can conduct a patdown for weapons. This applies even if the occupant is not suspected of any crime.[1] Courts recognize the inherent danger of traffic stops and provide officers with wide discretion when it comes to officer safety.

REPORT WRITING

1. Articulate any conduct by the passenger that caused officer safety concerns:

    a. Furtive movements

    b. Hostile/argumentative behavior

    c. Previous history/interactions

2. Articulate why you thought the passenger may be armed:

    a. Driver was found with weapon

    b. Passenger is known gang member

    c. You see bulge in their jacket, consistent with firearm

    d. You observe firearm indicia near passenger, like bullets

    e. Passenger makes statement that implies they are armed

3. Finally, state something like, "Based on the totality of the circumstances, I believed that the passenger may be armed and dangerous. For officer safety purposes, I conducted a patdown for weapons...).

4. Err on the side of your safety.

---

[1] Arizona v. Johnson, 555 U.S. 323 (U.S. 2009)

Patdown of Passenger Compartment

If you have reasonable suspicion that there is a weapon inside a vehicle, and that any of the occupants pose a danger, you may search anywhere in the passenger compartment where that weapon could reasonably be located.[1]

Report Writing

1. Articulate why you thought one of the occupants was dangerous:

    a. Past criminal history

    b. Investigating a crime involving violence

    c. Subject's words and actions

2. Articulate why you believe there may be a weapon inside the vehicle:

    a. Gun stickers

    b. Subject possesses a CCW

    c. Past criminal history involving weapons

    d. Member of a gang

3. Articulate how one of the occupants could gain access to the weapon:

    a. Not handcuffed

    b. Handcuffed, but near the vehicle

    c. Detained away from vehicle, but you anticipate occupant will reenter vehicle after stop

---

[1] Mich. v. Long, 463 U.S. 1032 (U.S. 1983)

4. If you found a weapon, or contraband in plain view, describe where you found it:

    a. You can search unlocked containers where weapon could be hidden (including other passenger's personal items)

    b. You can search locked containers if the suspect has a key

    c. You cannot search trunk unless you have P/C there is evidence or contraband or reasonable suspicion that the weapon is inside the trunk and the occupant has immediate access (usually because they have a key). Also, remember most newer vehicles have keyless trunk buttons and can be opened instantly. Articulate that fact if appropriate.

CASE EXAMPLES

Protective sweep upheld despite stopping wrong suspects

"Based on information obtained during the investigation of a series of armed robberies of drug dealers, law enforcement officers used "felony stop" tactics to stop a vehicle under the belief that it carried armed and dangerous suspects for whom arrest warrants had been issued. Although the specific suspects sought by the officers were not in the vehicle, the officers handcuffed and secured defendant and his passenger. ...A protective search yielded a pistol and ammunition, and a record's check indicated that defendant was a prior felon." Based on the totality of the circumstances protective search was reasonable.[1]

Traffic stops are inherently dangerous

"A police officer in today's reality has an objective, reasonable basis to fear for his or her life every time a motorist is stopped. Every traffic stop is a confrontation. The motorist who is stopped must suspend his or her plans and anticipates receiving a fine or perhaps even a jail term. That expectation becomes even more real when the motorist or a passenger knows there are outstanding arrest warrants or current criminal activity that may be discovered during the course of the stop."[2]

---

[1] United States v. Holmes, 376 F.3d 270 (4th Cir. S.C. 2004)
[2] United States v. Dennison, 410 F.3d 1203 (10th Cir. Colo. 2005)

Patdown of Citizens Riding in Police Vehicle

Whether you can patdown a citizen depends on why they are in your vehicle. If you're being nice and giving someone a ride home (e.g. mom and kids on freezing day) then you must seek consent. If, on the other hand, you had no choice but to transport them (e.g. take driver off highway after accident) then you may conduct patdown for weapons.

Guidelines

Keep these rules in mind:

1. If the ride is a courtesy, then seek consent.[1] If consent is refused, then you probably shouldn't provide the ride;

2. If the ride is a legal obligation, then seek consent. If consent is refused conduct a very limited search for weapons.[2] Alternatively, you could place purses and backpacks in trunk and not search them.

Case Examples

Policy requiring patdown of all lawfully transported suspects lawful

In cases where the police may lawfully transport a suspect to the scene of the crime in the rear of a police car, the police may carry out a departmental policy, imposed for reasons of officer safety, by patting down that person.[3]

---

[1] People v. Scott, 16 Cal. 3d 242 (Cal. 1976)
[2] People v. Tobin, 219 Cal. App. 3d 634 (Cal. App. 1st Dist. 1990)
[3] United States v. McCargo, 464 F.3d 192 (2d Cir. N.Y. 2006)

Constructive Possession

If you discover contraband inside a vehicle with multiple occupants and no one wants to claim ownership, you may charge multiple occupants with constructive possession.[1]

Alternatively, you could choose which occupant is the most culpable (usually the driver) and only charge him. Nothing requires that you arrest everyone under constructive possession. If you could arrest all, you can arrest one.

REPORT WRITING

Articulate the following:

1. Where the contraband was found relative to the occupants;

    a. On center console, in plain view

    b. On back seat, in plain view, etc.

2. Why a reasonable person would know the contraband was in the car;

    a. Strong odor inside passenger compartment

    b. Drug transaction occurred while occupants inside car

    c. Bolt cutters in plain view, etc.

3. Articulate any other facts or circumstances that would lead a reasonable person to believe that the arrested occupant would benefit from the contraband:

    a. Previous criminal history

    b. Admissions during the stop, like, "Yeah, I smoked [drugs] yesterday."

[1] Maryland v. Pringle, 540 U.S. 366 (U.S. 2003)

c. Stolen property and occupant has no gainful employment.

CASE EXAMPLES

All suspects involved in a hand-to-hand transaction were lawfully arrested

Two officers observed three suspects, in two vehicles, exchanging objects between their vehicles. Based on reasonable suspicion that they witnessed a hand-to-hand transaction, they made a stop. Drugs were eventually located and the court upheld the arrest of all suspects based on collective possession, even though the drugs were only found in one vehicle.[1]

Associate can be arrested when he willfully and knowingly exercises control

It is well-established that one need not actually possess the controlled dangerous substance to violate the prohibition against possession thereof, as constructive possession is sufficient. The mere presence in an area where drugs are located or the mere association with one possessing drugs does not constitute constructive possession, a person may be deemed to be in joint possession of a drug which is in the physical custody of a companion, if he willfully and knowingly shares with the other the right to control it.[2]

Boyfriend who stayed with girlfriend had constructive possession of full-auto AK47

Defendant argues that the officer did not have probable cause to believe that he actually or constructively possessed the firearm. He asserts that the bedroom where the AK-47 was found belonged to his girlfriend, and there was no evidence at the time of the arrest that he had knowledge of its existence. The court disagreed because defendant stayed at apartment, and suspiciously sat on bed when asked about the firearm.[3]

---

[1] United States v. Lopez, 441 Fed. Appx. 910 (3d Cir. Pa. 2011)
[2] Eyer v. Evans, 2004 U.S. Dist. LEXIS 1266 (E.D. La. Jan. 28, 2004)
[3] United States v. Brooks, 270 Fed. Appx. 382 (6th Cir. Ohio 2008)

Search of Vehicle Incident to Arrest

If you arrest any vehicle occupant, you may search the vehicle incident to arrest if the suspect has access to the vehicle.[1] You can search for evidence, contraband, weapons, or means of escape.

What does it mean for the suspect to have "access" to the vehicle? Generally, this means that the suspect is within lunge distance, and at the time of search they are unrestrained. Once the suspect has no reasonable access to the vehicle, then this exception no longer applies. For example, once the suspect is secured in a police vehicle you can no longer automatically search the vehicle incident to arrest.[2]

REPORT WRITING

Articulate the following:

1. The arrestee was an occupant of the vehicle;

2. The search incident to arrest occurred while he was within lunge distance;

3. The search sought evidence, contraband, weapons, or means of escape;

4. You can search any container within the passenger compartment (not trunk) including containers belonging to other occupants;[3]

5. You cannot search non-arrested occupants;[4]

6. This search exemption is scrutinized, and should be rare.

---

[1] New York v. Belton, 453 U.S. 454 (U.S. 1981)
[2] Arizona v. Gant, 556 U.S. 332 (U.S. 2009)
[3] Wyo. v. Houghton, 526 U.S. 295 (U.S. 1999)
[4] United States v. Di Re, 332 U.S. 581 (U.S. 1948)

Search of Vehicle Incident to 'Non-Custodial' Arrest

If you issue a citation in lieu of arrest, you don't get the "benefit" of conducting a search incident to arrest. For example, let's say that you find drug paraphernalia or misdemeanor possession of drugs and decide to release the person with a citation, it would be unlawful to search the suspect for more drugs even though you have probable cause. This is despite the fact that in many states you could just as easily arrest the person and then conduct a search incident to arrest. If you believe there is evidence inside the vehicle, you may search it with probable cause. But you couldn't search the suspect's person without consent or arrest.

GUIDELINES

If you issue a citation in lieu of arrest, you cannot search the suspect unless you have consent. Generally, traffic stops are treated as detentions, not arrests.[1]

CASE EXAMPLES

Search after issuing speeding ticket unlawful

Defendant was stopped by a police officer for speeding and was issued a citation rather than arrested. The officer then conducted a full search of defendant's car, incident to the citation. The officer found a bag of marijuana and a "pot pipe." Defendant was then arrested and charged with violation of Iowa state laws dealing with controlled substances. The Supreme Court held the search unlawful, since the officer did not arrest the defendant or gain consent.[2]

---

[1] People v. Brisendine, 13 Cal. 3d 528 (Cal. 1975)
[2] Knowles v. Iowa, 525 U.S. 113 (U.S. 1998)

Search for Evidence After Arrest

If you arrest any vehicle occupant and have reason to believe evidence of the crime is inside the vehicle, you can search the vehicle without a warrant. Two things should be noted. First, "reason to believe" evidence is inside the vehicle is a slightly lower standard than probable cause. And second, it doesn't matter if the suspect doesn't have immediate access to the vehicle. This search must be conducted contemporaneously with arrest.

REPORT WRITING

Articulate the following:

1. Articulate why you had reason to believe evidence would be located in the vehicle;

2. State that a warrantless search was conducted in order to retrieve the evidence contemporaneously with the arrest.

3. If you had probable cause that evidence was in the vehicle, you don't need to independently justify the search as contemporaneous to arrest because the search could be conducted based on the mobile conveyance exception.

CASE EXAMPLES

Officer can search vehicle if reasonable to believe evidence in vehicle

An officer is permitted to conduct a vehicle search when an arrestee is within reaching distance of the vehicle or it is reasonable to believe the vehicle contains evidence of the offense of arrest.[1] Note, you can still conduct a probable cause or inventory search if appropriate.

---

[1] Arizona v. Gant, 556 U.S. 332 (U.S. 2009)

Search of Vehicle with Probable Cause

If you have probable cause that a vehicle contains evidence or contraband, you can typically conduct a warrantless search.[1]

There are two reasons why the Supreme Court allows these searches:

1. Ready mobility of the vehicle means evidence could leave the jurisdiction before obtaining a warrant; and

2. Vehicles have a lowered reasonable expectation of privacy because they are heavily regulated.

REPORT WRITING

Articulate the following:

1. Probable cause that evidence or contraband is inside the vehicle;

2. The vehicle is readily mobile with little to no repair;[2]

    a. This includes out of gas, flat tire, dead battery

3. You had lawful access to the vehicle;

    a. You can conduct warrantless search inside impound yard

    b. Vehicles inside curtilage require warrant or exigency

4. Your search did not exceed the scope of the item sought.[3]

    a. If probable cause is for a particular container, don't search other containers[4]

---

[1] Md. v. Dyson, 527 U.S. 465 (U.S. 1999)
[2] Carroll v. United States, 267 U.S. 132 (U.S. 1925)
[3] United States v. Ross, 456 U.S. 798 (U.S. 1982)
[4] Cal. v. Acevedo, 500 U.S. 565 (U.S. 1991)

Vehicle Inventories

You may conduct an inventory search whenever you impound a vehicle. The main purpose of the inventory is very specific, to protect your agency from false allegations about stolen or damaged property. These inventories are searches, but they are not for evidence. Of course, plain view applies.

You cannot use vehicle inventories as a pretext to search a vehicle for contraband. This behavior is unlawful and can result in the suppression of evidence and 1983 lawsuits. Officers have discretion about whether or not to impound a vehicle, but they cannot tow a vehicle with the purpose of doing an "inventory." In other words, officers cannot use inventories as a loophole to the probable cause requirement.[1] Additionally, some states require police to give on-scene owners the opportunity to take possession of their vehicle, if feasible, instead of towing it.[2]

It would be lawful if your inventory policy permitted breaking open locked containers. But I do not recommend this approach. First, breaking containers open is going to backfire publicly and result in bad relations with your community. Second, in order to be constitutional, you must apply your inventory policy evenly. That means if you break open one container, you need to break open all containers. If not a defense attorney will show that you just conducted a warrantless search, not an inventory. If you really want inside a locked container, develop probable cause or get consent.

GUIDELINES

There are two important requirements for inventory searches:

1. Must have a written inventory policy which minimizes officer discretion;

---

[1] Colorado v. Bertine, 479 U.S. 367 (U.S. 1987)
[2] Commonwealth v. Naughton, 2003 Mass. Super. LEXIS 65 (Mass. Super. Ct. 2003)

2. Policy must spell out when inventories can be conducted and what areas can be searched.

Don't write in your report that you impounded a vehicle primarily so you could search it for contraband. It's okay to have a hunch that a vehicle may have drugs hidden in it, but remember you can't inventory for those reasons. Keep those thoughts out of your report! Just focus on legitimate reasons for towing the vehicle, like unlicensed driver, unregistered, involved in an accident, and so forth. If you find drugs, then simply articulate plain view.

CASE EXAMPLES

Officer admitted that inventory was a ruse to search

The narcotics team wanted Defendant stopped on a traffic offense, and deputies stopped him for failing to signal a turn. Upon determining that Torres was an unlicensed driver, they impounded his truck. The lead deputy testified that he was "basically using the inventory search as the means to go look for whatever narcotics-related evidence might be in" the truck. He did not establish any "community caretaking function warranting the impoundment." The court suppressed three pounds of methamphetamine, cocaine, a rifle, and over $113,000 in cash found in defendant's home.[1]

Officer open locked suitcase during inventory

During an inventory search an officer forced open a locked suitcase and found drugs. The Supreme Court suppressed the contraband because the agency's written policy did not tell officers that they could break open locked containers.[2]

Officer had tow driver unlock door

An officer towed a car that had been illegally parked. The car was locked and the officer saw non-incriminating items inside the vehicle. He asked the tow driver to open the car and the officer continued his inventory. Drugs were found in the glovebox and the owner was charged. The Court upheld the inventory.[3]

---

[1] People v. Torres, 188 Cal. App. 4th 775 (Cal. App. 4th Dist. 2010)
[2] Florida v. Wells, 495 U.S. 1 (U.S. 1990)
[3] South Dakota v. Opperman, 428 U.S. 364 (U.S. 1976)

Dangerous Item(s) Left Inside Vehicle

If you have reason to believe a dangerous item was left inside a vehicle which may endanger public safety if left unattended, you may seize the item for safekeeping.

REPORT WRITING

Articulate the following:

1. Describe your reason to believe that a dangerous item is inside an unattended vehicle (usually a gun); and

2. Describe why it would be a danger if left unattended.

CASE EXAMPLES

Warrantless search for gun upheld

Chester Dombrowski was a Chicago officer who was drunk and involved in a one-car traffic accident while driving a rental car in Wisconsin. He identified himself as a Chicago officer to the investigating officers, who understood that Chicago police officers were supposed to carry their weapons at all times. Dombrowski had no weapon on him, and none was found in the passenger compartment. They had the car towed to a private garage several miles from the police station. Dombrowski was arrested for drunk driving and then taken to the hospital. One of the officers returned to the car to retrieve Dombrowski's service revolver. While looking for it, the officer found evidence which strongly suggested that Dombrowski was involved in a crime of violence. When confronted with the evidence, he gave the location of a body. He was ultimately convicted of first degree murder.[1]

---

[1] Cady v. Dombrowski, 413 U.S. 433 (U.S. 1973)

Felony Eluding is a Violent Felony

In recent years, the Supreme Court has come down clearly on the side of law enforcement in their attempt to end dangerous vehicle pursuits. This includes classifying felony eluding as a violent felony for federal sentencing guidelines.

Report Writing

If a fleeing suspect is driving in such a manner that puts other drivers in danger, and if your state classifies such eluding as a felony, then for Fourth Amendment purposes the suspect is likely engaged in a violent felony. This classification is important not only for sentencing purposes, but also provides officers with wider use of force options, including the use of deadly force where appropriate in order to terminate the pursuit.

Whenever any force is used during a pursuit, the officer's report must articulate why that force was reasonable under Graham v. Connor standards.[1]

Case Examples

Felony eluding is a violent felony, narrow holding

Felony vehicle flight is a violent felony for purposes of the Armed Career Criminal Act.[2]

---

[1] Graham v. Connor, 490 U.S. 386 (U.S. 1989)
[2] Sykes v. United States, 564 U.S. 1 (U.S. 2011)

Deadly Force During Pursuit

Whether or not, as a matter of practice, police can use deadly force to end a dangerous pursuit has not been completely settled by the Supreme Court.[1] Still, the few cases that have been decided by the Court have been decided in the police's favor.

However, even if the Court unambiguously decided that police could use deadly force to end any dangerous pursuit, best police practices must be considered. I doubt the general public would endorse riddling a suspect's car with an AR-15 every time a suspect fled.

The Supreme Court cannot prevent suspects and innocent people suing you and your agency.

REPORT WRITING

If deadly force is used to end a dangerous pursuit, articulate the following:

1. Describe the original offense;

2. Articulate *every* fact or circumstance that made the pursuit dangerous:

    a. Speed and conduct or driver

    b. Other drivers, officers and pedestrians were put at risk

    c. Pre-knowledge that once pursuit ended suspect would be a deadly force threat

3. How the force used did not unreasonably put innocent people at risk. Generally, this does not include adult occupants in the suspect's vehicle, but does include children in the vehicle.

---

[1] Plumhoff v. Rickard, 134 S. Ct. 2012 (U.S. 2014)

Search Warrants

Search Warrant Overview

There are four specific core requirements of a search warrant. If any of these elements are later found to be missing the evidence found will likely be suppressed.

REPORT WRITING

The four requirements of a search warrant are:

1. Must establish probable cause within the affidavit, cannot add information later;

2. Must be supported by oath or affirmation;

3. Must particularly describe the place to be searched; and

4. Must particularly describe the item(s) or person to be seized.

CASE EXAMPLES

Warrant must be described with particularity

The uniformly applied rule is that a search conducted pursuant to a warrant that fails to conform to the particularity requirement of the Fourth Amendment is unconstitutional. That rule is in keeping with the well-established principle that except in certain carefully defined classes of cases, a search of private property without proper consent is unreasonable unless it has been authorized by a valid search warrant.[1]

---

[1] Groh v. Ramirez, 540 U.S. 551 (U.S. 2004)

Search Warrant Protection

A search warrant is given significant deferential treatment by the courts. In other words, if you take the time to obtain pre-authorization from a neutral and detached magistrate before conducting a search or seizure, the defendant will have to prove that the warrant was invalid.

This is no easy task. The defendant would usually have to prove that the officer was plainly incompetent or reckless with their facts, and that an objectively reasonable officer would know that the warrant did not establish the necessary probable cause.

GUIDELINES

For a search warrant to be held invalid, the defendant would need to prove:

- The magistrate was not neutral or detached; or

- The search warrant did not particularly describe the place to be searched or the things to be seized; or

- The officer was plainly incompetent or reckless with his facts; and

- An objectively reasonable officer would know that the warrant did not establish the necessary probable cause.

CASE EXAMPLES

Courts grant search warrants great deference

An officer got a warrant to search a suspected gang member's house for firearms. The trial court later found that the warrant was defective. However, the Supreme Court held that because the officer acted in good faith and was not "plainly incompetent" the exclusionary rule did not apply.[1]

---

[1] Messerschmidt v. Millender, 132 S. Ct. 570 (2011)

Anticipatory Search Warrant

An anticipatory search warrant is where probable cause will be established once a "triggering event" occurs. For example, the triggering event could be whenever an occupant, unknown at the time, receives a parcel known to contain narcotics.

REPORT WRITING

Articulate the following:

- Describe the facts and circumstances known thus far;

- Articulate why you believe a "triggering event" will occur in the near future; and

- Describe why that triggering event, combined with the other facts and circumstances, will equal probable cause to either enter a home to make the arrest and/or search for evidence.

CASE EXAMPLES

Supreme Court upholds anticipatory warrants

"When an anticipatory warrant is issued, the fact that the contraband is not presently located at the place described in the warrant is immaterial, so long as there is probable cause to believe that it will be there when the search warrant is executed."[1]

---

[1] United States v. Grubbs, 547 U.S. 90 (U.S. 2006)

Detaining a Residence

Generally, you may "freeze" or "detain" a residence if there's probable cause to believe there's evidence inside, and exigent circumstances exist that the evidence will be gone before receiving a search warrant.[1]

Under plain view, you may make a warrantless seizure of the evidence and leave (without conducting a further search while inside the residence). But often the best practice is to leave the evidence inside the residence, exclude the occupants, and obtain judicial approval with a warrant.

Remember, knock and announce rules apply.

REPORT WRITING

Articulate the following:

1. Describe your probable cause that evidence is inside the residence;

2. Articulate how and why the evidence may be destroyed or removed before obtaining a search warrant;

3. If you enter the residence, describe how you complied with knock and announce rules;

4. You may look in places where people could be hiding, do not look for evidence! Anything in plain view should be left and described in your search warrant;

5. Articulate how you sealed and secured the residence and diligently pursued a search warrant in order to not deprive the occupants of their property longer than necessary.

---

[1] Illinois v. McArthur, 531 U.S. 326 (U.S. 2001)

Knock and Announce

Whenever you enter a person's home without their consent, you must meet the requirements of knock and announce.[1] This applies whether you enter with a warrant or under a recognized exception. For example, even if you plan to enter a home because of a medical emergency, you are required to knock and announce before making a non-consensual entry unless an exception to knock and announce applies.

GUIDELINES

Reasons for knock and announce:

1. The protection of the privacy of the individual in his home;

2. The protection of innocent persons who may also be present on the premises where an arrest is made;

3. The prevention of situations which are conducive to violent confrontations between the occupant and individuals who enter his home without proper notice;

4. The protection of police who might be injured by a startled and fearful homeowner;[2] and

5. To avoid the unnecessary "destruction or breaking of any house."[3]

Exceptions to knock and announce:

1. The officer's presence is already known to the occupant;

2. The safety of the officer or others would be jeopardized by the announcement;

3. Delay caused by announcement would allow suspect to escape;

---

[1] Wilson v. Ark., 514 U.S. 927 (U.S. 1995)
[2] People v. Peterson, 9 Cal. 3d 717 (Cal. 1973)
[3] Wilson v. Ark., 514 U.S. 927 (U.S. 1995)

4. During hot pursuit; and

5. When the announcement may cause the evidence to be destroyed.

REPORT WRITING

Elements of knock and announce:

1. Police must "notify" the occupants of their presence. This is usually done by knocking but includes door bell, telephone, bullhorn, etc.

2. Police must announce their "authority" and "purpose." This is usually done by yelling, "Police, search warrant!"

3. Police must wait a reasonable time before making forced entry. Reasonable is usually based on how long it would take to destroy the evidence.[1]

Violations of knock and announce:

- Evidence found after a knock and announce violation won't be suppressed during trial (unless the violation was particularly shocking).[2] However, violations can result in discipline and 1983 lawsuits.

CASE EXAMPLES

Opening screen door, before announcement, was a knock and announce violation

Officers walked up to the residence to serve a search warrant and observed that the front door was open, along with a closed screen door. The lead officer knocked several times but did not announce his identity and purpose. He then opened the screen door and walked into the home, while announcing their identity and purpose. The court found this to be a violation of knock and announce. Still, the evidence was not subject to suppression.[3]

---

[1] United States v. Banks, 540 U.S. 31 (U.S. 2003)
[2] Hudson v. Michigan, 547 U.S. 586 (U.S. 2006)
[3] People v. Peterson, 9 Cal. 3d 717 (Cal. 1973)

Patdown of Occupants

You cannot *automatically* patdown every occupant present during the execution of a search warrant. The standard for a patdown remains the same: individualized reasonable suspicion that a person is armed and dangerous.

Fortunately, this standard is not difficult to meet, especially because search warrants can be inherently dangerous in the sense that occupants know exactly where the weapons are inside the residence and no officer would be able to watch the occupant 100% of the time. This "home court advantage" can help justify conducting a patdown.

The purpose of the warrant itself can also be a significant factor. Naturally there's different officer safety considerations if you're looking for a handgun versus tax records. But remember that mere presence at the scene of the warrant may not be sufficient, the occupant should be directly connected with the location. For example, if you were executing a search warrant at a bar known for dealing drugs, this would not provide independent justification for patting down (for weapons or drugs) every patron that happens to be there.[1]

REPORT WRITING

1. Some warrants provide sufficient justification to patdown occupants that are directly connected with the residence:

    a. Warrant is for weapons

    b. Search of violent suspect's home

    c. Known gang member residence

    d. Drug dealer's residence

    e. Most "no knock" warrants

---

[1] Ybarra v. Ill., 444 U.S. 85 (U.S. 1979)

2. If the patdown is based on independent justification, articulate why:

    a. Prior violent history

    b. Known gang member

    c. Furtive movements

    d. Bulge consistent with firearm

    e. You see a weapon, like pocket knife

3. Plain view (feel) applies.

CASE EXAMPLES

Police cannot search people simply because they are at the house

Persons detained during a search for evidence cannot be searched simply because they are there. Accordingly, those officers who conducted indiscriminate searches of all persons present at the family residences failed to act in an objectively reasonable manner, and are not entitled to qualified immunity.[1]

Patdown usually authorized of narcotics dealers

Courts tend to recognize the likelihood that narcotics suspects are often armed and may allow a patdown with no more than the conclusory opinion that the "need for officer safety" dictated the need for a patdown.[2]

Can't conduct patdown because it's "the safe thing to do"

During a probation search an officer cannot patdown a present known associate, even when there's evidence of drug abuse occurring at the house, just because it is "the safe thing to do." Officers still need individualized suspicion that a particular person is armed.[3]

---

[1] Marks v. Clarke, 102 F.3d 1012 (9th Cir. Wash. 1997)
[2] People v. Samples, 48 Cal. App. 4th 1197 (Cal. App. 1st Dist. 1996)
[3] People v. Sandoval, 163 Cal. App. 4th 205 (Cal. App. 3d Dist. 2008)

Detaining Individuals Present

Generally, you can detain individuals who are on-scene for the duration of the search warrant.[1] Courts recognize the officer safety concerns during a warrant execution and why it's important to maintain absolute control of the residence.

The best practice would be to detain only the following individuals:

- The home's occupants so they can open locked containers or otherwise assist in an orderly search of the residence;

- Any individual who will likely be arrested as a result of the search;

- Any individual who would present an officer safety issue if released (gang members or other hostile people);

- Any other individual for good cause.

I strongly recommend that you don't needlessly detain uninvolved individuals not listed above, especially children. This is a best practice and makes law enforcement appear more professional and reasonable.

REPORT WRITING

Articulate why occupants were detained:

- In order to open locked containers or otherwise assist in the orderly search of the residence;

- Subject would likely be arrested as a result of the search;

- Subject posed an officer safety issue and therefore was controlled during the execution of the search warrant;

[1] Mich. v. Summers, 452 U.S. 692 (U.S. 1981)

- Subject was detained for other good cause;

- Don't detain mere customers at a business.

CASE EXAMPLES

Visitors may be detained briefly during probation/parole search

A probation officer may lawfully "briefly" detain a visitor in a house who is present in the house of a juvenile probationer during a Fourth wavier search long enough to determine whether he is a resident of the house or is otherwise connected to illegal activity.[1]

14-hour detention/interrogation of party-goers unreasonable

A sheriff's investigator was held **not** to be protected by qualified immunity when sued for detaining partygoers for as long as 14 hours after a warrant search for evidence of illegal gaming was executed. Interrogating the participants is not part and parcel of executing a warrant. Also, the detentions could not be justified as Terry stops because individualized suspicion was not established by the partygoers' mere presence in the same large mansion where some limited drug and gaming contraband was discovered, and because detentions as long as 14 hours did not remotely resemble the brief detention authorized by Terry v. Ohio.[2] Note, this search warrant was executed by SWAT and yielded two non-functioning slot machines and 3 grams of pot! Whoops.

Authority to detain is categorical

An officer's authority to detain incident to a search is categorical; it does not depend on the quantum of proof justifying detention or the extent of the intrusion to be imposed by the seizure.[3] Note, the Supreme Court still requires that the duration of detention be reasonable. Over-detention is still unreasonable.

---

[1] People v. Rios, 193 Cal. App. 4th 584 (Cal. App. 5th Dist. 2011)
[2] Guillory v. Hill, 233 Cal. App. 4th 240 (Cal. App. 4th Dist. 2015)
[3] Muehler v. Mena, 544 U.S. 93 (U.S. 2005)

Detaining Suspect Who Comes to Residence During S/W

If a suspect came to the residence during the execution of a search warrant, they may be detained if they appear involved in the crime at issue.

REPORT WRITING

In order to detain articulate the following:

- What was the reason for the search warrant;

- Why you believe that the suspect that came upon the residence during the search warrant was, or is, involved in the crime at issue, for example:

  o Serving a drug warrant and individual likely showed up to buy drugs

  o Serving a stolen property warrant and individual likely showed to either sell more stolen property, or buy stolen property

- Release the suspect if you dispel your suspicions or convert the detention into a consensual encounter.

CASE EXAMPLES

Lawful detention of subject who arrived on-scene of large marijuana grow operation

Subject likely knew about grow operation, and used a code to enter the facility.[1]

---

[1] United States v. Davis, 530 F.3d 1069 (9th Cir. Or. 2008)

Detaining Occupants Outside the Residence

Generally, you cannot detain occupants who have left the residence. There are two notable exceptions:

1. The occupant was detained immediately after they left their residence, and are within the "immediate vicinity."[1]

2. The occupant was briefly detained after leaving the residence to:

   a. Retrieve keys to the residence in order to eliminate damage;

   b. Inform the occupant that you are going to serve a warrant on the residence and ask if they would help open locked containers or otherwise assist in the recovery of the evidence in order to reduce damage and time spent at the residence. If the occupant declined, and you are not going to make a P/C arrest, let the occupant go.

REPORT WRITING

1. Describe how occupant was within the immediate vicinity;

2. If there are other occupants in the residence who may destroy evidence, articulate that the occupant was detained as close to the residence as possible, but not within line of sight in order to prevent destruction of evidence;

3. Describe the ease of reentry if not detained (officer safety issue);

4. Other relevant factors (undefined by Court).

---

[1] Bailey v. United States, 133 S. Ct. 1031 (U.S. 2013)

Handcuffing

You cannot *automatically* handcuff subjects present during the execution of a search warrant. Like patdowns, you must have an articulable reason before applying any restraints. Remember, courts consider handcuffs a use of force and the mere presence during the execution of a search warrant may not call for using force. Naturally, you can use handcuffs whenever you execute a dangerous search warrant.[1] Best practices require that if prolonged restraints are required (e.g. more than an hour or so) then other accommodations should be considered so that restraint-based injuries don't occur.

Further, prolonged detentions may require bathroom breaks and access to water. Courts may find the initial detention reasonable, but the method (prolonged handcuffing) unreasonable. You should constantly re-evaluate whether or not restraints are still necessary.

REPORT WRITING

1. Articulate why a subject was handcuffed:

    a. High-risk warrant

    b. Search warrant for weapons

    c. Subject tried to flee

    d. Previous history with suspect

2. Always articulate that you checked for tightness and double-locked. If subject complains of injury, recheck handcuffs;

3. Articulate that continued use of restraints was considered throughout the execution of the warrant. If restraints were removed, articulate when and why in your report.

---

[1] Muehler v. Mena, 544 U.S. 93 (U.S. 2005)

Sealing Affidavits

Typically, you are supposed to leave a copy of the search warrant, including affidavit, during the search warrant execution. Unfortunately, this may compromise your investigation. You're allowed to seal a search warrant <u>affidavit</u> for "good cause." You can seal the affidavit for a specific number of days, or after a court order.

REPORT WRITING

Articulate why you want to seal the affidavit. Permissible reasons may include:

- The sealing of the affidavit is necessary to protect an informant or witness;

- Disclosure of the information will compromise an on-going investigation;

- The suspects under investigation might destroy evidence, coordinate their stories before testifying before the grand jury, or flee the jurisdiction if the information is disclosed.

CASE EXAMPLES

Federal courts have inherent discretion to seal affidavits

The district court has the inherent power to seal affidavits filed with the court in appropriate circumstances. "The government contends that the materials should be sealed to protect the informant and to keep confidential ongoing investigations. We find that, on this basis, the district court did not abuse its discretion." [1]

---

[1] United States v. Mann, 829 F.2d 849 (9th Cir. Or. 1987)

Wrong Address Liability

Whenever police execute a search warrant at the wrong house there is likely to be a lawsuit. How much is paid usually depends on three factors:

1. Lack of pre-warrant due diligence;

2. Amount of damage to residence or injuries to occupants; and

3. Police conduct once they knew, or should have known, they were at the wrong address.

It's vital that before you seek a search warrant, especially one involving SWAT, you conduct a quality investigation and verify the address. Most mistakes can be corrected before the warrant is sought.

It's vital that once police realize they hit the wrong house they immediately begin to correct or diminish the injury caused.[1]

REPORT WRITING

Articulate the following:

1. Describe the pre-warrant investigation;

2. Articulate why it was reasonable to believe the suspect or evidence was at that address;

3. Describe what police did to minimize the damage or injury once it was realized it was the wrong address.

---

[1] L.A. County v. Rettele, 550 U.S. 609 (U.S. 2007)

Technology Searches

Sensory Enhancements

Generally, you can use sensory enhancements if they are in general public use (like binoculars and flashlights). But, you must be reasonable, especially when you use technology to see inside protected areas. If not your actions could be classified as a warrantless search requiring exigent circumstances.

REPORT WRITING

If you use a sensory enhancement device without a warrant in order to gain information about a protected area (e.g. person, house, business, etc.) you should articulate the following:

1. Describe the <u>sophistication of the device</u>. The less sophisticated the device the more likely it will be reasonable;

2. Describe <u>where the device was used</u>. If the device was used to view things in public, it will probably be considered reasonable. If the device was used to search a protected area (like a house), you'll need to articulate why the device did not violate a reasonable expectation of privacy; finally,

3. Describe whether or not the <u>device is in general public use</u>. The more the public uses the device, the more reasonable it is that police can use it for investigations.

Electronic Surveillance

Electronic surveillance will most likely be a search or seizure protected under the Fourth Amendment if it occurred in protected areas (i.e. house or car) or where a person has a reasonable expectation of privacy (i.e. email account).

The Supreme Court has struggled to keep up with the times with technological advancement. However, there Court is beginning to see just how intrusive modern technology can become, and is limiting use of technology in investigations. Generally, be very cautious with electronic surveillance, and try to err on the side of getting a search warrant unless there's legitimate exigency.

CASE EXAMPLES

Use of beeper tracking was lawful

Agents hid a beeper (today a GPS) in a can of ether. The defendant bought the ether (for use in a drug lab) and agents tracked it back to his house. Based on the information, agents got a search warrant. The Court found that once the can was brought into the house the defendant had a reasonable expectation of privacy.[1] But the tracking information outside the home was admissible.

---

[1] United States v. Karo, 468 U.S. 705 (U.S. 1984)

Thermal Imaging

Generally, you cannot use thermal imaging to look at protected areas, like homes or private areas of a business. You could use thermal imaging in public areas, like open fields or parks. If you want to use thermal imaging on a house you need consent, exigent circumstances, or a warrant. My advice is to get a warrant.

GUIDELINES

- If you use a thermal imager on a <u>house or private area of a business, you need consent, exigency or a warrant</u>. An example of exigency could include use by a SWAT team to ascertain where a suspect is located;

- If you use a thermal imager on an <u>area where there isn't a reasonable expectation of privacy</u>, like a park or public area of a business, describe that in your report.

CASE EXAMPLES

Cannot use a thermal imager against a home, without warrant

When the police use a thermal imager to gain any information regarding the interior of the home that could not otherwise have been obtained without physical intrusion, that constitutes a search.[1]

Police may use thermal imager in open fields

"[T]he officers in this case were entitled to observe the steel building either by air or on foot because the building, like the barn in Pace, stood in an open field. And, as we have already discussed, the fact that the officers enhanced their observations with a thermal imager does not require a different conclusion."[2]

---

[1] Kyllo v. United States, 533 U.S. 27 (U.S. 2001)
[2] United States v. Ishmael, 48 F.3d 850 (5th Cir. Tex. 1995)

Flashlights

Generally, you can use flashlights to enhance your vision. There are two good reasons for this. First, the Supreme Court stated that evidence visible during the day would not get additional protections simply because it was concealed by darkness. Second, flashlights are in "general public use" and the public expects police officers to use them, wherever a police officer has a lawful right to be.

Still flashlights can violate a person's reasonable expectation of privacy if the flashlight is used in an unreasonable manner. Take, for example, a police officer who is conducting a knock and talk. It would be unlawful to shine a high-powered LED flashlight through closed blinds in order to illuminate inside the home. On the other hand, if the blinds were open, then a person would lose their reasonable expectation of privacy and enhancing your view with a flashlight would be lawful.

Report Writing

Public areas

If you use your flashlight to observe unprotected areas (like outside of buildings, abandoned property, etc.), then you don't need to articulate additional information.

Protected areas

If you used your flashlight to illuminate inside a protected area, like inside a house or private area of a business, you may be required to articulate how you did not violate any reasonable expectation of privacy. One way to do this is to articulate that what you saw with your flashlight would have been seen unaided if viewed in the day.

Night Vision Goggles

There is no particular restriction if you use night vision goggles. They fall under the same rules as flashlights. However, some prosecutors and judges may not understand this technology and may equate it with thermal imaging, which is very restricted.

REPORT WRITING

Some judges or prosecutors may misunderstand night vision technology and believe it has the same capability as thermal imaging. Therefore, articulate that night vision goggles simply amplify the ambient light and do not detect any heat signatures.

SAMPLE LANGUAGE

"At approximately 1 a.m. I was conducting undercover surveillance on 123 Main Street. I was parked on Oak Drive, approximately 100 yards from the target residence. Due to low light conditions, I could not see the suspects who were in the front yard. I utilized night vision goggles, which amplified the ambient lighting and works like an invisible flashlight."

CASE EXAMPLES

Night vision goggles the same as a flashlight

"It was dark the entire time he was there. While he did not use a flashlight, the deputy wore "night vision" goggles during both this visit and a subsequent visit. The goggles enhanced the available light by magnifying it, allowing him to see better in the dark. The goggles merely amplify ambient light to enable one to see something that is already exposed to public view."[1]

---

[1] People v. Lieng, 190 Cal. App. 4th 1213 (Cal. App. 1st Dist. 2010)

Binoculars

You can use binoculars to enhance your vision to view items or people if they are in a public place, such as parks, sidewalks or streets.[1] You cannot, however, use binoculars to view items or people inside private areas that would otherwise be completely indistinguishable by the naked eye. For example, if you were investigating a jewelry heist and you saw a "gold glint" coming through the suspect's open apartment window, you could lawfully use binoculars to *confirm* what you saw.[2]

On the other hand, it would be unlawful to use binoculars to peer into a suspect's apartment window from 200-300 yards away to determine whether he was viewing child pornography. In this case, there was no way an officer could see any incriminating evidence with the naked eye and therefore the suspect does not lose his reasonable expectation of privacy.[3]

REPORT WRITING

Articulate the following:

Protected areas: If you use binoculars to look into protected areas (houses, tents, garages) you must first articulate that the item was somewhat <u>visible with the naked eye</u>. For example, "I saw a TV inside the suspect's garage and after using binoculars I confirmed that the TV was the same make and size as the one stolen."

Non-protected areas: You can use binoculars to look at any area where a <u>person doesn't have a reasonable expectation of privacy</u> (parks, public businesses, open fields). It doesn't matter that you couldn't see the incriminating item without the enhancement.

---

[1] United States v. Shepard, 1995 U.S. App. LEXIS 23118 (9th Cir. Ariz. 1995)
[2] Cooper v. Superior Court, 118 Cal. App. 3d 499 (Cal. App. 1st Dist. 1981)
[3] People v. Arno, 90 Cal. App. 3d 505 (Cal. App. 2d Dist. 1979)

Sample Language

"I was parked on a public street near Smith's home approximately 200 yards away. I observed with the naked eye an object in Smith's right hand that had the approximate shape and size of a handgun. Smith fully extended his right arm straight in front of his body, and pointed the object towards his TV. I used 10x50 binoculars and confirmed that Smith was holding a black handgun, similar to a Glock. A previous record's check confirmed that Smith is a convicted felon, and therefore prohibited from possessing a firearm."

Case Examples

Use of binoculars from open field not a Fourth Amendment search

"At the trial, Special Investigator Griffith testified that through binoculars, he observed the appellant, a known liquor violator, placing two large cardboard boxes (each of which contained six gallons of untaxed whiskey), in a 1961 Buick. The observations were made from a field belonging to another, about 50 yards from the appellant's house. This did not constitute an illegal search."[1]

Use of high-power telescope to see inside a hotel room an unlawful search

Police made a binocular search of a hotel room through the uncurtained window by means of a powerful telescope on a hilltop a quarter of a mile from the hotel. There were no buildings or other locations closer to the hotel from which anyone could see into the hotel room. By using the telescope, the police observed a well known gambling sheet. The court held the defendant had a reasonable expectation that no one could see into his room under these circumstances: "[I]t is inconceivable that the government can intrude so far into an individual's home that it can detect the material he is reading and still not be considered to have engaged in a search."[2]

---

[1] United States v. Grimes, 426 F.2d 706 (5th Cir. Ga. 1970)
[2] United States v. Kim, 415 F. Supp. 1252 (D. Haw. 1976)

Cell Phones, Laptops and Tablets

You cannot search cell phones without consent, exigency or a search warrant. This includes searches incident to arrest, even where you have probable cause that evidence of the crime is contained on the phone. The Supreme Court no longer includes cell phones as part of the "search incident to arrest" exception. This rule applies to all devices that can contain "vast amounts of personal data," like laptops and tablets.

Valid exigency would include looking in an active shooter's cell phone to determine if there were undiscovered accomplices. Or looking in a kidnapper's cell phone if the victim has not been found.

REPORT WRITING

If you search a cell phone, laptop or tablet you need either consent, exigency or a search warrant. Note, if you or conducting an inventory search and simply hit the power button on a device to verify it works, that would not be a "search." If you saw crime related evidence on the lock screen (like gangbanger/felon with gun), you could use that in a search warrant.

CASE EXAMPLE

Defendant was stopped for a traffic violation, which eventually led to his arrest on weapons charges. An officer searching Riley incident to the arrest seized a cell phone from defendant's pants pocket. The officer accessed information on the phone and discovered evidence of gang activity, which led to evidence of a shooting a few weeks earlier. The Court found the warrantless search unreasonable since mobile devices hold a vast amount of personal data. [1]

---

[1] Riley v. California, 134 S. Ct. 2473 (U.S. 2014)

Aerial Surveillance

Generally, police are not prohibited from flying an aircraft over protected areas, like a person's home and backyard.[1] Anything observed falls under plain view and may be used in a search warrant.

There are three notable exceptions: First, police should not violate FAA rules unless there are exigent circumstances, such as tracking a fleeing suspect. Second, the manner of flight shouldn't be highly intrusive, like a loud helicopter hovering directly over the home, or multiple passes over the home, otherwise the manner of the surveillance may become unreasonable.[2] Third, police are permitted to use "moderate enhancement" to view the protected area. It may help to review the guidelines on flashlights, binoculars, and thermal imaging. Overall, if your conduct is reasonable, then it's likely lawful.

REPORT WRITING

If you conduct aerial surveillance over unprotected areas, like open fields, then no additional explanation is necessary. If the surveillance was conducted over a protected area, like a home, you should articulate how your actions were not overly intrusive.

CASE EXAMPLES

Available technology helps determine what is reasonable

"It would be foolish to contend that the degree of privacy secured to citizens by the Fourth Amendment has been entirely unaffected by the advance of technology. For example,...the technology enabling human flight has exposed to public view (and hence, we have said, to official observation) uncovered portions of the house and its curtilage that once were private."[3]

---

[1] Cal. v. Ciraolo, 476 U.S. 207 (U.S. 1986)
[2] People v. Mayoff, 42 Cal. 3d 1302 (Cal. 1986)
[3] Kyllo v. United States, 121 S. Ct. 2038 (U.S. 2001)

GPS Trackers

You cannot attach a GPS tracker to a vehicle without consent, exigency, or warrant. An example of exigency is if you found a kidnapper's vehicle in a parking lot and needed to immediately track it back to the victim's location.

REPORT WRITING

Exigency:

1. Articulate the seriousness of the crime at issue;

2. Describe why there was no time to get a search warrant;

3. Get a search warrant as soon as practicable.

CASE EXAMPLES

Warrantless attachment of GPS to vehicle unlawful

Agents installed a GPS tracking device on the undercarriage of a vehicle registered to defendant's wife while it was parked in a public parking lot. Over the next 28 days, the Government used the device to track the vehicle's movements. The U.S. Supreme Court determined that the Government's installation of the GPS device on defendant's vehicle, and its use of that device to monitor the vehicle's movements, constituted a "search."[1]

Tracking suspect through their cellphone GPS is a Fourth Amendment search

Warrantless GPS tracking constitutes a search even in the absence of a trespass, because a Fourth Amendment search occurs when the government violates a subjective expectation of privacy that society recognizes as reasonable.[2]

---

[1] United States v. Jones, 132 S. Ct. 945 (U.S. 2012)
[2] State v. Brereton, 2013 WI 17 (Wis. 2013)

Digital Passwords

If you need a defendant's digital password after he asserts his 5th Amendment rights, good luck. If the password is in the defendant's head, then courts will likely refuse to compel the defendant to provide the password because it would be viewed as testimony, and therefore protected.[1]

However, if the phone can be opened with a fingerprint, then get a court order. Fingerprints are physical evidence unprotected by the Fifth Amendment.

GUIDELINES

Generally, you cannot order a defendant to provide a digital password if they have invoked their 5th Amendment rights.

CASE EXAMPLES

Cannot compel suspect to provide password to computer

Compelled testimony that communicates information that may "lead to incriminating evidence" is privileged even if the information itself is not inculpatory.[2]

Suspect may be compelled to unlock device with fingerprint

Defendant cannot be compelled to produce his passcode to access his smartphone but he can be compelled to produce his fingerprint to do the same.[3]

---

[1] United States v. Kirschner, 823 F. Supp. 2d 665 (E.D. Mich. 2010)
[2] Doe v. United States, 487 U.S. 201 (U.S. 1988)
[3] Commonwealth v. Baust, 89 Va. Cir. 267 (Va. Cir. Ct. 2014)

Medical Searches

Cause of Injury Searches

You're allowed to conduct a limited "medical search" of an unconscious person or someone in serious medical distress in order to determine the cause of injury (if unknown) and to ascertain their identification.

Your search should be objectively reasonable under the circumstances, and not a ruse to simply look for contraband. An example of a lawful search would be a victim who was found unconscious and there were no clear signs why. It would be lawful to look for a medical alert bracelet, identification, medicines, or even illegal drugs they may have overdosed on in order to provide that information to medical. Any contraband or evidence found in plain view could be admitted into evidence.

REPORT WRITING

If a victim was unconscious or in medical distress you can conduct a medical search for their cause of injury. It's important to articulate this in your report, especially if you find contraband in plain view. Remember, you're not "searching for evidence." Instead, your intention is to help the victim by informing medical what the cause of injury is.

CASE EXAMPLE

Police may make warrantless "community caretaking" searches
The Supreme Court, in upholding the warrantless search of a vehicle, made specific reference to the necessity for local police to engage in "community caretaking functions, totally divorced from the detection, investigation, or acquisition of evidence relating to the violation of a criminal statute."[1]

---

[1] Cady v. Dombrowski, 93 S. Ct. 2523 (U.S. 1973)

Breath Tests

The courts do not view DUI breath tests and blood tests the same. A blood test, because it is naturally more invasive, usually requires a search warrant absent exigent circumstances. As the Supreme Court pointed out in Birchfield;

> "A breath test does not 'implicat[e] significant privacy concerns.' Blood tests are a different matter. ... Blood tests are significantly more intrusive, and their reasonableness must be judged in light of the availability of the less invasive alternative of a breath test. ... Breath tests have been in common use for many years. Their results are admissible in court and are widely credited by juries, and respondents do not dispute their accuracy or utility....

> Nothing prevents the police from seeking a warrant for a blood test when there is sufficient time to do so in the particular circumstances or from relying on the exigent circumstances exception to the warrant requirement when there is not.

CASE EXAMPLE

Officer may order a suspect submit to breath test after an arrest

"Because breath tests are significantly less intrusive than blood tests and in most cases, amply serve law enforcement interests, we conclude that a breath test, but not a blood test, may be administered as a search incident to a lawful arrest for drunk driving. As in all cases involving reasonable searches incident to arrest, a warrant is not needed in this situation."[1]

Note: If suspect refuses to blow, that refusal can be used against them in court.

---

[1] Birchfield v. North Dakota, 136 S. Ct. 2160 (U.S. 2016)

Blood Draws

If you have consent, exigent circumstances, or a search warrant you may conduct a blood draw in a medically approved manner. If you have exigent circumstances[1] or a search warrant, you may use reasonable force to hold down the suspect while medical personnel obtains the blood sample.

REPORT WRITING

If you have consent, describe how the consent was voluntarily given.

If you have exigency, you must articulate that the evidence (drugs or alcohol) normally dissipates and that there was no time to apply for a search warrant:

- Driver is going to be flown out of area or state for treatment;

- Prolonged time to arrive on scene;

- Driver was combative;

- Articulate the seriousness of the crime (DUI with death)

CASE EXAMPLE

Blood draws invoke the Fourth Amendment

"Intrusions into the human body, including the taking of blood, are searches subject to the restrictions of the Fourth Amendment."[2]

---

[1] Missouri v. McNeely, 133 S. Ct. 1552 (U.S. 2013)
[2] United States v. Wright, 215 F.3d 1020 (9th Cir. Cal. 2000)

Attempts to Swallow Drugs

Sometimes a suspect will try to swallow drugs before you arrest them. "A suspect has no constitutional right to destroy or dispose of evidence by swallowing, consequently he cannot consider the mouth a 'sacred orifice' in which contraband may be irretrievably concealed from the police."[1]

If possible, you should prevent the drugs from going inside their mouth, but if that doesn't work I suggest you don't place your hands around the subject's throat. Some courts have held this practice per se excessive force.[2] You are under no legal obligation to retrieve drugs that the suspect tries to swallow. The only liability would be not summoning medical aid.

I suggest let him swallow the drugs and transport him to the hospital. Let the professionals figure it out. In the end, it's worth losing a possession case then catching the Alphabet Soup (HIV/Hep). Is that worth preventing a "victimless crime?"

REPORT WRITING

1. What led you to believe the suspect swallowed contraband;

2. What you did in response. Remember, you're under no legal obligation to physically respond and I suggest you don't. Articulate in your report that drug users commonly have communicable diseases, may bite, and for everyone's safety you did not try to retrieve the digested items and instead called for medical (if the suspect can't breathe do the Heimlich); and

3. No matter what, let medical make the decisions. For example, don't tell the doctor that you would like the suspect's stomach pumped in order to retrieve the evidence. You would need a warrant for that. If you're unable to retrieve the evidence you still

---

[1] State v. Williams, 16 Wn. App. 868 (Wash. Ct. App. 1977)
[2] People v. Jones, 209 Cal. App. 3d 725 (Cal. App. 1st Dist. 1989)

have P/C to arrest for obstruction, tampering with evidence, and so forth.

Sample Language

As I began to arrest Doe for possession of narcotics he reached into his right front pocket and removed a small plastic baggie, which I believed contained narcotics. He began to insert the baggie into his mouth and I immediately grabbed Doe's right arm in an effort to prevent destruction of evidence and a drug overdose.

My attempt was unsuccessful and Doe inserted the object into his mouth. I then ceased my attempt to retrieve the evidence. In my training and experience drug users may have communicable diseases and if I continued my efforts I may have had direct contact with Doe's saliva, or may have been bitten.

I observed Doe for any airway obstructions and called for medical. Once medical arrived I told them what occurred and allowed them to make all necessary medical decisions. After treatment, Smith was booked into jail. (whether or not evidence was retrieved.)

Case Example

Ordering a suspect to spit out drugs reasonable

Because officers, who had probable cause to believe that defendant had just put illegal drugs in his mouth, had no way of knowing how it was packaged, and thus whether it would be destroyed by ingestion or would pass through his body, they were presented with exigent circumstances and were permitted to order him to spit out the drugs.[1] Note, the officers did not grab the suspect's neck.

Applying hands to a suspect's throat is the equivalent of choking

"That type of force, more than any other, is likely to result in violent resistance by the arrestee, and should be disapproved as a police technique. An application of force to the throat sufficient to prevent swallowing is, in our opinion, the equivalent of choking."[2]

---

[1] State v. Alverez, 111 P.3d 808 (Utah Ct. App. 2005)
[2] People v. Trevino, 72 Cal. App. 3d 686 (Cal. App. 2d Dist. 1977)

Intrusions in the Body

If you have probable cause that a suspect has swallowed evidence, or has contraband in their anal or vaginal cavities, you'll need to consult with medical personnel to retrieve it. Rarely will you have exigent circumstances to retrieve it yourself (why would you want to?) For example, if a corrections officer discovered partially concealed contraband during a visual strip search, it would be unlawful to retrieve it. The officer would either have to request the inmate remove it himself (if it was safe to do so), or contact medical.

If an arrestee swallowed evidence (like drugs) and it created a medical emergency, no search warrant would be required as long as medical personnel made all decisions, including not retrieving the evidence and allowing the person to metabolize the drugs.

If no medical emergency exists, and you want to retrieve the evidence, you must seek a search warrant (very unlikely).

REPORT WRITING

Warrant articulation:

1. Describe the seriousness of the crime, the more serious the crime the more likely a warrant may be approved;

2. Articulate exactly what evidence you're looking for and why it is vital for your investigation;

3. Describe the medical procedure and risks (the lower the better);

4. Explain that police will make no medical decisions; and

5. Finally, describe that the procedure will be carried out in a manner that affords the suspect proper privacy and dignity.

Post-report articulation:

1. Describe the extend of resistance by the suspect, and any force used;

2. Articulate that the force you used did not threaten the suspect's health or interfere with medical personnel; and

3. Finally, describe everything you did to carry out the procedure with dignity and respect for the suspect. For example, private room, transporting handcuffed suspect through backdoor, allowing suspect to ask doctor questions, and so forth. Courts want to see you weren't barbaric in carrying out the medical procedure.

CASE EXAMPLES

If police request medical staff to recover evidence, then Fourth Amendment applies

"When a medical procedure is performed at the instigation of law enforcement for the purpose of obtaining evidence, the fact that the search is executed by a medical professional does not insulate it from Fourth Amendment scrutiny."[1]

Surgical intrusions for evidence will rarely be approved

"A compelled surgical intrusion into an individual's body for evidence implicates expectations of privacy and security of such magnitude that the intrusion may be unreasonable even if likely to produce evidence of a crime."[2]

Unless there's legitimate exigency, you must seek a warrant

"Search warrants are ordinarily required for searches of dwellings, and, absent an emergency, no less could be required where intrusions into the human body are concerned. The importance of informed, detached and deliberate determinations of the issue whether or not to invade another's body in search of evidence of guilt is indisputable and great."[3]

---

[1] Sanchez v. Pereira-Castillo, 590 F.3d 31 (1st Cir. P.R. 2009)
[2] Winston v. Lee, 105 S. Ct. 1611 (U.S. 1985)
[3] Schmerber v. Cal., 86 S. Ct. 1826 (U.S. 1966)

Discarded DNA

A person has no reasonable expectation of privacy in an item that has their DNA which they later discard. For example, if suspect drinks from a cup and throws it away, you can test it for DNA as long as you had lawful access to the cup (for example, restaurant trash). Since the suspect has no privacy in the cup there's no Fourth Amendment search.

Report Writing

1. First describe why you are testing the DNA. Though not required, courts want to know that police are not conducting mass surveillance of innocent people by gathering their DNA;

2. Next describe how the suspect attached their DNA to a particular item, and how that item was not contaminated by other subjects. For example, if you saw the suspect drinking out of a coffee cup describe that no one else drank from the same cup;

3. Finally, describe where the item was discarded and how you had lawful access to retrieve the item. Also, describe how the DNA wasn't contaminated after being discarded. Preferably, the item would not be mixed in with trash before being retrieved.

Case Examples

Discarded cigarette butt abandoned

There was not Fourth Amendment violation when defendant voluntarily discarded his cigarette butt by tossing it onto a public sidewalk and left it in a place particularly suited for public inspection. He thus abandoned the cigarette butt in a public place and had no reasonable expectation of privacy concerning the DNA testing of it to identify him as a suspect in a murder. [1]

---

[1] People v. Gallego, 190 Cal. App. 4th 388 (Cal. App. 3d Dist. 2010)

Fingernail Scrapes

If you have reasonable suspicion or probable cause to believe a suspect committed a crime, and currently has evidence underneath their fingernails, you can conduct a warrantless "scrape" and retrieve any evidence such as dirt, blood, DNA and so forth. You're allowed to use the minimal force necessary to recover the evidence.

REPORT WRITING

1. Articulate what reasonable suspicion or probable cause you had against the suspect;

2. Describe why you thought evidence was under the suspect's fingernails (visible foreign material);

3. If you asked for consent, share whether it was granted or denied;

4. Either way, articulate that the warrantless search could have been conducted for two reasons; fingernail scrapes are a very limited intrusion and the ready destructibility of the evidence.

CASE EXAMPLE

Officer permitted to conduct fingernail scrape during arrest
Where there is probable cause, a very limited intrusion undertaken incident to a station house detention, and a ready destructibility of evidence, a warrantless search of a defendant's fingernails does not violate the Fourth Amendment.[1]

---

[1] Cupp v. Murphy, 412 U.S. 291 (U.S. 1973)

Right to Cross Examine Forensic Analyst

Generally, a defendant has a Sixth Amendment right to cross examine the forensic analyst if their evidence is introduced at trial. The Supreme Court found that providing a substitute analyst was not acceptable. The defendant had the right to cross-examine the actual analyst who inspected the evidence.

CASE EXAMPLES

Defendant has a right to cross-examine crime lab personnel

At defendant's trial, a substitute analyst from the same laboratory testified concerning the testing device and the laboratory's testing procedures. The prosecution contended that the reporting analyst only transcribed the machine-generated test results. The U.S. Supreme Court held that admission of the report of defendant's blood alcohol level violated defendant's right to confront the analyst who prepared the report. The report was clearly testimonial in nature as a statement made in order to prove a fact at defendant's criminal trial, and the testimony of the substitute analyst who did not perform or observe the reported test did not satisfy the right to confrontation. Further, the report did not consist exclusively of a machine-generated information but also indicated that the analyst properly received defendant's sample, performed testing on the sample adhering to protocol, and observed no circumstance or condition affecting the integrity of the sample or the validity of the analysis, and the substitute analyst could not convey what the reporting analyst knew or observed, or expose any lapses or inaccuracies on the part of the reporting analyst.[1]

---

[1] Bullcoming v. New Mexico, 564 U.S. 647 (U.S. 2011)

Schools

School Searches

The Fourth Amendment applies to public school employees. In T.L.O., the Supreme Court held that warrantless searches in schools fall under the "special needs" doctrine. The Court held that public school officials do not need search warrants or probable cause to search for and seize evidence from students under their authority. Instead, student searches may occur if they are "reasonable" under all the circumstances as (1) justified at their inception and (2) reasonable in scope.[1] The key for school officials is to articulate everything in a written report.

Lockers

Students have little reasonable expectation of privacy in their lockers. Some factors courts may consider is whether the student was informed that lockers could be searched at any time, whether the school provided the lock, and whether the locker contents could be viewed without opening it (e.g. mesh door). Locker searches based on general or individualized suspicion will be upheld. Random and suspicionless locker searches will be judged on a case by case basis and officials should articulate the need to maintain a safe campus and why students would not have a reasonable expectation of privacy in their locker.

Desks and work areas

Students and staff members have no reasonable expectation of privacy in areas that are shared with others. Additionally, this applies to hallways, classrooms, and school computers.

Vehicles on School Grounds

School officials can run a drug K9 on the outside of vehicles without reasonable suspicion.[2] However, officials need individualized suspicion

---

[1] New Jersey v. T.L.O. 105 S.Ct. 733 (U.S. 1985)
[2] Myers v. State, 806 N.E.2d 350 (Ind. Ct. App. 2004)

in order to conduct a warrantless search for drugs, firearms, or evidence of school policy violations.

Metal Detectors and Bag Searches

Metal detectors and student bag searches upon entry to a school is considered a special needs search and will be upheld without reasonable suspicion.[1]

Searches of Student Social Media Accounts and Cell Phones

Officials may surf the internet and view publicly available information. However, compelling a student to provide a Facebook password likely violates the First and Fourth Amendments.[2] Officials cannot search a student's confiscated cell phone absent reasonable suspicion that criminal activity or violation of school policy would be found.[3]

Strip Searches

Strip searches are highly intrusive and should only be done if absolutely necessary. If possible, arrest the juvenile and have the detention center conduct the search. If that is not an option, and it's imperative that the evidence be recovered, conduct the search in the most delicate and professional manner possible. Same sex searcher, private, and use professional language at all times. Consider recording the encounter with a body cam, but hold hand over camera to block any view of private areas (i.e. keep recording audio).

Field Trips

The lowered standard applies to off-campus field trips.

REPORT WRITING

Articulate the following:

1. What information or circumstances led the school official to believe that a student was committing, or about to commit, a school violation or crime;

2. How the warrantless search or seizure was reasonable in scope, relative to the need to maintain a safe and structured environment;

---

[1] People v. Pruitt, 278 Ill. App. 3d 194 (Ill. App. Ct. 1st Dist. 1996)
[2] R.S. v. Minnewaska Area Sch. Dist. No. 2149, 894 F. Supp. 2d 1128 (D. Minn. 2012)
[3] G.C. v. Owensboro Pub. Sch., 711 F.3d 623 (6th Cir. Ky. 2013)

3. If a SRO was involved, and the search was based on reasonable suspicion, articulate how the SRO was an <u>agent</u> of the school official.

CASE EXAMPLES

School searches only require a "moderate chance" of finding evidence

The lesser standard for school searches could as readily be described as a moderate chance of finding evidence of wrongdoing.[1]

Purse Search

A teacher at a New Jersey high school found a 14-year-old freshman smoking cigarettes in a school lavatory in violation of a school rule, and took them to the Vice Principal's office. The student denied that she had been smoking and claimed that she did not smoke at all. The Vice Principal demanded to see her purse. Upon opening the purse, he found cigarettes and rolling papers that are commonly associated with the use of marijuana. He then proceeded to search the purse and found some marijuana, a pipe, plastic bags, a fairly substantial amount of money, an index card containing a list of students who owed the student money, and two letters that implicated her in marijuana dealing. The search was constitutional.[2]

Strip Search for Prescription Ibuprofen Illegal

A school principle made a warrantless search of a student's belongings because she apparently possessed over the counter ibuprofen. The search included telling the student to pull out the elastic on her underwear in order to release any contraband that may have been hidden there. The Supreme Court found this "strip search" unreasonable and a violation of the Fourth Amendment.[3]

Search of Shoes Not Strip Search

A search of socks and shoes for stolen money was not a strip search.[4]

---

[1] Safford Unified Sch. Dist. #1 v. Redding, 129 S. Ct. 2633 (U.S. 2009)
[2] New Jersey v. T.L.O. 105 S.Ct. 733 (U.S. 1985)
[3] Safford Unified Sch. Dist. #1 v. Redding, 557 U.S. 364 (U.S. 2009)
[4] Wynn v. Board of Education, 508 So. 2d 1170 (Ala. 1987)

SRO's

When the Supreme Court issued its opinion in T.L.O.[1] which authorized warrantless searches based on reasonable suspicion instead of probable cause, school resource officers were rare. In fact, the Court noted that the official's search of the students purse for cigarettes may have been different if the search was conducted by a police officer.

But today SRO's are common and the question is whether or not the lower Fourth Amendment standard applicable to school searches applies to SRO's. The short answer appears to be no; police are still held to the higher probable cause standard. But things get a little more confusing when the SRO and school official work together. Which standard applies? Read guidelines below, that should help.

GUIDELINES

Police give information to school officials
If police learn of criminal activity, and relay that information to school officials, the reasonable suspicion standard applies.

School officials give information to police
If school officials learn of criminal activity and call police for assistance, and ask officers to conduct the search on the school's behalf, then the reasonable suspicion standard applies. The key here is that the police are acting as the school's agent. If the police "take over" the investigation, then the regular rules apply.

Police conduct a criminal investigation, with the help of school officials
If the school asks that the police take over the criminal investigation, or the SRO intends to file criminal charges based on his investigation, then apply the regular rules. At the end of the day, try to use common sense. If the search is primarily a school search, then T.L.O. applies. If

---

[1] New Jersey v. T.L.O. 105 S.Ct. 733 (U.S. 1985)

the search is primarily a criminal investigation, apply full Fourth Amendment protections.

CASE EXAMPLES

Officers can perform patdown, but not full search on truant student

Two police officers came into contact with the juvenile. at a government housing project behind a high school. The officers believed she was truant, so they stopped her. She appeared to be 16 or 17-years old and wore a polo shirt bearing the high school emblem. After confirming she should be in school, they told her they were going to transport her back there. Before placing her in the police car, one of the officers, searched all of her pockets and found a small bag of marijuana. Court held that officers were permitted to conduct a patdown, but not a full search.[1]

Officer who searched student at dance required probable cause

An officer at a school dance required probable cause before searching a student who smelled of alcohol. The lower reasonable suspicion standard did not apply because the officer was acting in a criminal investigation capacity.[2]

Reasonable suspicion standard applied to SRO

A SRO helped school officials investigate a fight. The SRO was acting as a school official at the time of the school search because "[h]e was on duty as an SRO and acting under his authority as an SRO when he personally observed the activity that formed the basis for his search."[3]

Probable cause not required merely because police are involved

School official's reasonable suspicion standard for search is not elevated to probable cause merely because the school official asks a police officer to help conduct the search.[4]

---

[1] L.C. v. State, 23 So. 3d 1215 (Fla. Dist. Ct. App. 3d Dist. 2009)
[2] State v. Tywayne H., 123 N.M. 42 (N.M. Ct. App. 1997)
[3] In re J.F.M. , 168 N.C. App. 143 (N.C. Ct. App. 2005)
[4] J.A.R. v. State, 689 So. 2d 1242 (Fla. Dist. Ct. App. 2d Dist. 1997)

School Drug Testing

Schools are allowed to conduct random, suspicionless, urinalysis of public school students who participate in extracurricular activities (primarily athletic). However, schools cannot conduct random drug testing of the entire student body. A school may require a student to submit to drug testing if they have reasonable suspicion of illegal drug use.

GUIDELINES

Schools may conduct random drug testing on students who participate in extracurricular activities because of the reduced expectation of privacy students have and to combat the severity of the drug problem in public schools. The manner of the testing must be reasonable and the results must be on a need-to-know basis.

It is imperative that school officials coordinate drugs testing with their attorneys. This is an area that could generate expensive lawsuits.

Checklist:

1. Articulate every fact and circumstance that led school officials to believe a student was under the influence of illegal drugs;

2. Interview the student, if possible, and attempt to gain an admission that the student consumed illegal drugs;

3. If the school chose to conduct a drug test, articulate why;

4. Articulate that any result, positive or negative, would be held confidential and on a "need to know" basis;

5. Finally, articulate how any test conducted was performed in a medically-approved and dignified manner.

Restraining Student Movement

Officials must be very cautious and hesitant whenever force is used against a child. If you use any force, make sure that it's absolutely necessary under the circumstances. Kids are not adults. And many times, it may be wise to allow the kid to yell and scream without restraining them if they are not a danger. You make the call, but remember that if you use force be able to articulate why.

REPORT WRITING

1. Articulate why force was <u>necessary</u>;

2. Articulate that force was not used to punish or embarrass the child, and once the need for force was over, restraints were removed (if applicable).

CASE EXAMPLES

Taping kid's head to tree unreasonable punishment

A teacher told a student to stand against a tree and stay there as punishment for fighting. The student did not stay still and the teacher taped the student's head to the tree. A factfinder could find that the official's conduct was objectively unreasonable because there was no indication that the student posed a danger to others, he was only eight years old, and the conduct was so intrusive that another fifth grader observed it was inappropriate.[1]

Handcuffing is not reasonable punishment

A SRO witnessed a child refusing to do jumping jacks and talking back to the coach. The deputy told her "this is what it feels like to be in jail" and handcuffed her. The court held that the deputy's action was excessive force.[2] Note, I can't make this stuff up.

---

[1] Doe v. Haw. Dep't of Educ., 334 F.3d 906 (9th Cir. Haw. 2003)
[2] Gray v. Bostic, 458 F.3d 1295 (11th Cir. Ala. 2006)

Private Schools

The Fourth Amendment does not apply to private school searches, even if the school receives most of their operating funds from public revenue. Therefore, any search conducted by a private school is admissible in evidence and not subject to the exclusionary rule.

Additionally, the lower T.L.O. reasonable suspicion standard does not apply to private schools. Police officers must apply regular Fourth Amendment protections.

CASE EXAMPLES

Private school search not bound by the Fourth Amendment

Defendant went on a school-sponsored ski trip. He and the other trip participants stayed at a resort hotel. Defendant and other students were aware that they were subject to certain rules, including the seizure of contraband either at school or on school trips. A chaperone learned that some students had been to their room unsupervised and investigated. He found marijuana and cocaine. The Defendant was arrested and argued that the school violated his rights. The court held that the school was not a government actor.[1]

---

[1] Commonwealth v. Considine, 448 Mass. 295 (Mass. 2007)

Special Searches

Mail Searches

You cannot search any first-class mail or package without a warrant. However, if you have lawful access you can read any writing on the outside of mail and packages.[1]

REPORT WRITING

1. Describe where the mailbox was and how you had lawful access to it (e.g. near sidewalk);

2. Describe what you saw (addresses) and share that you did not open any sealed envelopes. State that the suspect did not have a reasonable expectation of privacy on the writings on the outside of a package.'

CASE EXAMPLES

No reasonable expectation of privacy in mail addressed to "alias"

Agents with the USPS became suspicious of a package. Inspectors found that both the sender and receiver's names did not match mail records. The investigation revealed that the actual intended recipient had the package sent to a friend's house under a fake name. The friend consented to allow police to search the package and narcotics were discovered. The intended recipient was arrested. The court found that since the recipient used a fake name and sent it to a friend's house, he did not have a reasonable expectation of privacy.[2]

Police may seize mail and apply for a warrant

Officers who have probable cause may seize a package and apply for a warrant.[3]

---

[1] United States v. Burnette, 375 F.3d 10 (1st Cir. N.H. 2004)
[2] State v. Williams, 184 So. 3d 1205 (Fla. Dist. Ct. App. 1st Dist. 2016)
[3] Garmon v. Foust, 741 F.2d 1069 (8th Cir. Iowa 1984)

Arson Investigations

Generally, warrants are required when investigators search for evidence in a protected area. However, firefighters are allowed to search for the "origin of a fire" in order to prevent a fire from restarting.[1]

Guidelines

Whether a post-fire search is OK depends on several factors:

1. Whether there are legitimate privacy interests in the damaged property (type of property, amount of damage);

2. Whether exigent circumstances exist (unknown cause of fire);

3. Whether object of the search is to gather evidence of a crime or determine cause of fire (here it needs to be the cause);

4. If access is denied, arson investigators can make warrantless entry to search for origin of fire. Otherwise, get a warrant.

Case Examples

Firefighters permitted to search house after waterbed broke

The defendant accidently caught his waterbed on fire, which in turn caused the waterbed to leak into the basement. Firefighters entered the basement in order to ascertain whether there was an electrical fire hazard (due to water leak). Firefighters found explosives in the basement and these observations were upheld as lawful.[2]

---

[1] Mich. v. Clifford, 464 U.S. 287 (U.S. 1984)
[2] United States v. Buckmaster, 485 F.3d 873 (6th Cir. Ohio 2007)

Airport Checkpoints

A person has a reduced expectation of privacy if they are attempting to access a secure area of an airport. Additionally, a person who has started the screening process cannot "opt-out" and leave.

GUIDELINES

Airport searches must follow these rules:

1. The search is made in good faith for weapons or explosives;

2. Passengers may avoid the search by electing not to fly, which must be done before placing luggage on x-ray conveyor belt.

CASE EXAMPLES

Passengers that enter screening area impliedly consented to search

The passenger was subjected to a random search, at an airport security checkpoint, of a carry-on bag that passed through an x-ray scan without arousing suspicion. Nothing was found in his bag and he proceeded to board the airplane. The passenger argued that random post-x-ray searches were unconstitutional, unless the x-ray scan aroused suspicion. The court held that the passenger impliedly consented to the random search by placing his bag on the x-ray conveyor belt.[1]

Airport screening must be limited to weapons and explosives

A particular airport security screening search is constitutionally reasonable provided that it "is no more extensive nor intensive than necessary, in the light of current technology, to detect the presence of weapons or explosives [and] that it is confined in good faith to that purpose."[2]

---

[1] Torbet v. United Airlines, Inc., 298 F.3d 1087 (9th Cir. Cal. 2002)
[2] United States v. Aukai, 497 F.3d 955 (9th Cir. Haw. 2007)

Border Searches

An exception to the warrant requirement developed for searches at the border or its functional equivalent because of the specific difficulties and governmental interests involved in border crossings and the problem of smuggling contraband, dutiable goods, and even illegal aliens.

Under the border search exception to the warrant requirement, neither probable cause, reasonable suspicion, nor a search warrant is required for a Customs or immigration search of persons, personal effects, belongings, or vehicles at the border or its functional equivalent. [1]

Who may conduct a border search?

Customs agents, Coast Guard officers, immigration officers, agriculture officers and Border Patrol officers are all Customs officials capable of conducting a border search. FBI agents and local police officers are not included. However, local officers are permitted to be present and assist a border search (See case below).

When can a border search be conducted?

Merely presenting oneself for entry is "gaining entry," and it is sufficient to warrant a border search, and one cannot attempt to decline entry to avoid it. [2] Additionally, a suspect who was turned around by Canadian border officials was found to be crossing the border, and subject to search. [3]

What is the scope of a border search?

Border searches can be as intense as the situation permits. [4] Officers may search persons, papers, computers, vessels, luggage, airplanes, mail, and packages. Strip searches are not authorized unless justified

---

[1] 2-35 Search and Seizure § 35.01 (2015)
[2] United States v. Cascante-Bernitta, 711 F.2d 36 (5th Cir. La. 1983)
[3] United States v. Serhan, 2015 U.S. Dist. LEXIS 72899 (E.D. Mich. June 5, 2015)
[4] 2-35 Search and Seizure § 35.10 (2015)

with articulable facts. Body cavity searches are only authorized in officers have a "clear indication" of smuggling (basically you can see it visually or via x-ray).

CASE EXAMPLES

State police trooper allowed to help with border search

Customs officials and a state trooper patrolled the Louisiana coast. Without any suspicion of criminal activity, they boarded a boat and conducted an inspection where they found bales of marijuana. The court found the search lawful under Fourth Amendment.[1]

Municipal guardsman not authorized to make border search

A suspect ran from a border search and was immediately caught by a municipal guardsman. The guardsman conducted a search and found cocaine which they handed over to an arriving customs agent. The court found the guardsman was not allowed to make searches on behalf of the customs agent. Still, the evidence was admitted under inevitable discovery doctrine.[2]

Miranda warnings not required

Miranda warnings are not required because it is considered a "routine administrative interview."[3]

Strip search must be justified

"[A]lthough anyone entering or leaving the country may expect to have his luggage and personal effects examined, he does not expect that his entry or departure, standing alone, will cause him to be subjected to a strip search. Before a border official may insist upon such an extensive invasion of privacy, he should have a suspicion of illegal concealment that is based upon something more than the border crossing, and the suspicion should be substantial enough to make the search a reasonable exercise of authority."[4]

---

[1] United States v. Villamonte-Marquez, 462 U.S. 579 (U.S. 1983)
[2] United States v. Brown, 858 F. Supp. 297 (D.P.R. 1994)
[3] United States v. Miller, 2009 U.S. Dist. LEXIS 62396 (E.D.N.Y. July 21, 2009)
[4] United States v. Asbury, 586 F.2d 973 (2d Cir. N.Y. 1978)

Probationer & Parolee Searches

Most probationers/parolees have a "search clause" that authorizes warrantless searches of their person, residence, car, and any property under their control at any time of day.

Additionally, police officers may conduct the search on behalf of the probation officer if the search is related to the probationer's status. These rules differ by state.

GUIDELINES

If the probation officer is not present and the search is done by police, the warrantless search is valid if:[1]

1. Authorized by a probation officer; and

2. Related to the suspect's probationary status.

- The probation officer should not be the "agent" of police

CASE EXAMPLES

Arrest of probationer inside doctor's office held unconstitutional

"The evidence, interpreted in the light most favorable to [plaintiff medical office manager], is sufficient for a jury to conclude that her Fourth Amendment rights were violated [by probation officer's unwarranted entry into medical office in search of probationer for whom arrest warrant had been issued]. Though physical entry of the home is the chief evil against which the wording of the Fourth Amendment is directed, its protection extends to any area in which an individual has a reasonable expectation of privacy. Offices and other workplaces are among the areas in which individuals may enjoy such a reasonable expectation of privacy."[2]

---

[1] United States v. Richardson, 849 F.2d 439 (9th Cir. Cal. 1988)
[2] O'Rourke v. Hayes, 378 F.3d 1201 (11th Cir. Fla. 2004)

Jails & Prisons

Visual Strip Search During Booking

Jails are allowed to conduct a visual strip search if the inmate is going to general population.[1] Also, a visual strip search may be conducted on an inmate if they were arrested on a drug related offense and there's reason to believe they have concealed contraband.

REPORT WRITING

Articulate the following if contraband was found:

1. A routine visual strip search was conducted because the inmate was going to enter general population after booking; or alternatively;

2. Articulate why it was reasonable to believe that the suspect may have hidden contraband on their person;

3. The manner of the strip search must be reasonable:[2]

    a. Search must be private

    b. Searcher of the same sex

    c. Must be hygienic conditions

    d. Should be little to no physical contact with inmate

    e. Staff must remain professional at all times (no jokes)

4. If contraband was discovered inside the inmate's orifice, ask the inmate to remove if it can be conducted safely; if the inmate says they cannot or refuses, involve medical staff.

5. Again, the search must be conducted by same sex officer.

---

[1] Florence v. Bd. of Chosen Freeholders, 566 U.S. 318 (U.S. 2012)
[2] Evans v. City of Zebulon, 351 F.3d 485 (11th Cir. Ga. 2003)

Body Cavity Search

Generally, officers cannot conduct a body cavity search without a search warrant or exigent circumstances.[1] Additionally, a body cavity search must be done in accordance with medically approved procedures and in sanitary conditions.[2] The overall search must be reasonable.

REPORT WRITING

1. Articulate probable cause that contraband is inside a body cavity;

2. Ask suspect to remove the item, if possible;

3. If you have exigent circumstances, you may involve medical staff in order to immediately retrieve the contraband (rare);

4. Apply for a search warrant:

    a. Articulate probable cause

    b. Articulate that search will be conducted:[3]

        1) In a private room

        2) By medical staff (any sex) and an officer of the same sex

        3) Under hygienic conditions

        4) There will be no physical contact between officer and inmate unless necessary to carry out procedure

        5) Procedure will be carried out in a professional and dignified manner

---

[1] Fuller v. M.G. Jewelry, 950 F.2d 1437 (9th Cir. Cal. 1991)
[2] Rodriquez v. Furtado, 771 F. Supp. 1245 (D. Mass. 1991)
[3] Evans v. City of Zebulon, 351 F.3d 485 (11th Cir. Ga. 2003)

DNA Swabs

Jail personnel may conduct a DNA swab on any suspect booked for a serious offense or felony.[1]

Guidelines

The Supreme Court considers a DNA swab the same as other routine booking activities, such as fingerprinting and photographing, but only for serious offenses or felonies.

Case Examples

DNA swabs implicates the Fourth Amendment

"The compulsory extraction of blood for DNA profiling unquestionably implicates the right to personal security embodied in the Fourth Amendment, and thus constitutes a search within the meaning of the Constitution. Of course, the fact that such extraction constitutes a search is hardly dispositive, as the Fourth Amendment does not proscribe all searches and seizures. It would be foolish to contend that the degree of privacy secured to citizens by the Fourth Amendment has been entirely unaffected by the advance of technology."[2]

---

[1] Maryland v. King, 133 S. Ct. 1958 (U.S. 2013)
[2] Ellison v. Nevada, 299 Fed. Appx. 730 (9th Cir. Nev. 2008)

Inmate Privacy in Mail

Generally, you can read all mail except legal mail. The logic here is that all mail coming in/out of the prison may contain contraband or communication about escape plans or threats.[1] You cannot read an inmate's communication with their lawyer.

Incoming mail
Officials can open all incoming mail (except legal) to search for contraband, escape plans, or evidence of any prison rule violations. Officials may censor mail if they articulate that it's "reasonable." This is a lower standard then censored outgoing mail. Inmates still retain First Amendment rights.

Outgoing mail
Officials may open outgoing mail to search for contraband, escape plans, threats and so forth. However, any censorship must further a substantial governmental interest.[2]

Legal mail
Officials cannot read or censor any mail that is from or to a lawyer. It's the responsibility of the sender (lawyer or inmate) to clearly mark the mail as legal mail. Legal mail doesn't include "jailhouse lawyers" or co-defendants.[3]

GUIDELINES

Follow these guidelines:

1. You may open and read all mail, except legal mail.

---

[1] Withrow V. Paff (9th Circuit, 1995)
[2] Procunier v. Martinez, 416 U.S. 396 (U.S. 1974)
[3] Vida v. Cage, 385 F.2d 408 (6th Cir. Mich. 1967)

2. In order for legal mail to be treated as confidential, it is the responsibility of the sender to mark it as legal (i.e. has attorney return address);

3. You may open legal mail in front of inmate to verify no contraband is inside envelope, but cannot read it;

4. You may restrict books, magazines and other materials if reasonably related to a government penological interest.

CASE EXAMPLES

Legal mail doesn't cover jailhouse lawyers

Inmate sought to restrain warden from interfering with the ability of the inmate and an individual portrayed as his "best friend" to assist each other concerning legal matters. The "best friend" was also in federal custody, but he was detained in another facility. The district court denied the inmates request.[1]

Unlawful destruction of mail addressed to paralegal

Prison officials intercepted and destroyed an inmate letter addressed to a paralegal seeking legal assistance. The court found that the letter was legitimate legal mail.[2]

Prisons can require specific language on outside of legal mail

A court upheld the requirement of federal prisons that legal mail contain the phrase, "Special Mail -- Open Only in the presence of the inmate" on the front of the envelope, along with the name of the attorney. Without this phrase, mail can be opened outside the presence of the inmate. Still, use common sense.[3]

Legal mail must be opened in front of the inmate

The prison's adherence of a rule whereby the inmate was present when mail from attorneys was inspected was all that the constitution required.[4]

---

[1] Wilkerson v. Warden of U. S. Reformatory, 465 F.2d 956 (10th Cir. Okla. 1972)
[2] Washington v. James, 782 F.2d 1134 (2d Cir. N.Y. 1986)
[3] United States v. Stotts, 925 F.2d 83 (4th Cir. N.C. 1991)
[4] Wolff v. McDonnell, 418 U.S. 539 (U.S. 1974)

Inmate Privacy in Cell

The Supreme Court has acknowledged that under certain circumstances a prisoner's cell is like their home away from home. Yet, when it comes to reasonable expectation of privacy the Court stated that prisoners have none. There's two noteworthy reasons. The first reason is that the prison has a compelling interest in keeping the prison safe. The other is that because all prisoners know their cell could be inspected at any time, it would not be subjectively reasonable for the prisoner to have an expectation of privacy.

GUIDELINES

A prisoner has no reasonable expectation of privacy in their prison or jail cell.

CASE EXAMPLES

Prisoners have no privacy in their cells

"The administration of a prison is at best an extraordinarily difficult undertaking. But it would be literally impossible to accomplish the prison objectives identified above if inmates retained a right of privacy in their cells. Virtually the only place inmates can conceal weapons, drugs, and other contraband is in their cells. Unfettered access to these cells by prison officials, thus, is imperative if drugs and contraband are to be ferreted out and sanitary surroundings are to be maintained."[1]

---

[1] Hudson v. Palmer, 468 U.S. 517 (U.S. 1984)

Delayed Release of Inmates

Jails or prisons must diligently release inmates after they have served their sentence or otherwise been properly released. An intentional delay can constitute grounds for a lawsuit or charges for false imprisonment.

However, in order to prove such a constitutional violation, the inmate must be able to prove that the defendant officers personally participated in his over-detention or that the over-detention was the result of a pattern or custom on the part of the law enforcement agency.[1]

GUIDELINES

Once an inmate is to be released, corrections personnel should diligently process the inmate out of the system.

---

[1] Avalos v. Baca, 596 F.3d 583 (9th Cir. Cal. 2010)

Use of Force

Non-Deadly Force

Whenever police use non-deadly force it must be objectively reasonable. The key is to articulate every material fact in the report. Police should not add important details later, otherwise it loses credibility. Here are some factors to consider:

- Suspect/officer ratio

- Suspect/officer size and ability differences

- Prior knowledge of suspect

- Presence and availability of weapons

- Physical positioning

- Environment

- Other subjects in area that are sympathetic to suspect

REPORT WRITING

1. How serious was the offense that the officer suspected was or had been committed?

2. Did the suspect pose a physical threat to the officer or some other person present at the scene?

3. Was the suspect actively resisting or attempting to evade arrest by flight?[1]

4. Reasonable force will be judged by the totality of the circumstances (articulate above factors).

---

[1] Graham v. Connor, 490 U.S. 386 (U.S. 1989)

Deadly Force

You may use deadly force in order to protect yourself or others from imminent or immediate serious bodily harm or death. Additionally, you may use deadly force to "arrest" a violent fleeing felon who would pose a significant risk to others if not captured immediately. You must give a warning, if feasible, before using deadly force.

Note that many courts are looking more closely at officer conduct leading up the ultimate need to use force. For example, an undercover officer ran towards the defendant with his gun drawn, in reaction the suspect pulled out his own firearm, causing the officer to shoot. The court found that the confrontation could have been avoided because there was a uniformed officer across the street who could have made contact with the suspect.[1]

REPORT WRITING

1. An officer may use deadly force when faced with an immediate or imminent danger of serious bodily harm or death to himself or another person on scene; or

2. An officer who has probable cause to believe that a fleeing suspect had been involved in a violent felony involving the infliction or threatened infliction of serious bodily harm or death may use deadly force. Additionally, the officer should articulate that if the suspect was allowed to escape innocent people could be faced with imminent serious bodily harm or death; and

3. Officers must give a warning, if feasible, before using deadly force;[2]

4. Reasonable force is judged by the totality of the circumstances.[3]

[1] St. Hilaire v. City of Laconia, 885 F. Supp. 349 (D.N.H. 1995)
[2] Tenn. v. Garner, 471 U.S. 1 (U.S. 1985)
[3] Graham v. Connor, 490 U.S. 386 (U.S. 1989)

Improper Handcuffing

Handcuffing is a *use of force* and therefore must meet the reasonableness requirements under Graham v. Connor. You can be held liable for excessive force if you improperly handcuff a suspect. Additionally, liability can be incurred if you fail to remove handcuffs when no longer necessary. Remember, handcuffs are *temporary* restraints.

REPORT WRITING

1. Articulate that you checked the handcuffs for appropriate tightness and double-locked them (prevent them from tightening during transport);

2. If a suspect complains that the handcuffs are too tight, check them again. Or have another officer check them. Add this to your report. The general rule is that suspects get one free check;

3. If a *compliant* suspect complains of an injury that could be aggravated by handcuffing them behind their back, handcuff them to the front if possible (even if your policy forbids it, call your supervisor and push the decision up the chain in order to reduce *your* liability).[1] This also applies to pregnant suspects or heavy-set suspects. At the very least, apply multiple sets of handcuffs so their arms are relatively separated.

CASE EXAMPLES

Suspect may go to trial over excessive force claim

The suspect complained that his handcuffs were on too tight. They remained on for an additional 15 minutes while being booked. He sued and the court held that claim could go to trial.[2]

---

[1] Aceto v. Kachajian, 240 F. Supp. 2d 121 (D. Mass. 2003)
[2] Martin v. Heideman, 106 F.3d 1308 (6th Cir. Ky. 1997)

Pointing Guns at Suspects

Officers should never point their firearm at anyone unless completely justified by a serious threat. First, an officer could have a negligent discharge (never good). Second, pointing guns during an investigative detention could result in a de facto arrest, requiring probable cause. Finally, courts have found that needlessly pointing guns at suspects may result in excessive force. Nothing good can come from needlessly pointing your firearm.

Naturally, un-holstering your firearm at the low ready is much different and usually doesn't result in liability if you can articulate a good reason.

Guidelines

1. If you point your firearm at anyone, articulate why you believed it was necessary for officer safety reasons. If not, you could be held liable for excessive force;[1]

2. Never purposefully target children with your firearm during a SWAT raid unless justified (higher standard than adults);

Case Examples

Holding children at gunpoint unreasonable

"While the SWAT Team's initial show of force may have been reasonable...continuing to hold the children directly at gunpoint after the officers had gained complete control of the situation outside the residence was not justified under the circumstances at that point. This rendered the seizure of the children unreasonable, violating their Fourth Amendment rights."[2]

---

[1] Robinson v. Solano County, 278 F.3d 1007 (9th Cir. Cal. 2002)
[2] Holland v. Harrington, 268 F.3d 1179 (10th Cir. Colo. 2001)

Patrol K9's

Generally, patrol canines are not considered deadly force, even if a suspect dies as a result of their deployment. However, a jury may find their use objectively unreasonable if a suspect was not given a warning and an opportunity to peacefully surrender before deploying a canine trained in the bite and hold method.

If no warning was given articulate why it was unreasonable, unsafe or impractical under the circumstances.

REPORT WRITING

Whenever you deploy a "bite dog," you should first give a warning to the suspect in order to provide an opportunity for the suspect to surrender peacefully. If no warning was provided, articulate why:

- The suspect was armed, and therefore an immediate deadly threat;

- Suspect was running and out of earshot range;

- Suspect was given a previous warning and refused to surrender.

CASES EXAMPLES

Trained bite dogs are not deadly force

The use of a patrol dog does not constitute deadly force.[1]

A warning should be given, if feasible, before releasing a bite dog

A jury can properly find that the failure to give a verbal warning before using a police dog trained to bite and hold is objectively unreasonable.[2]

---

[1] Robinette v. Barnes, 854 F.2d 909 (6th Cir. Tenn. 1988)
[2] Kuha v. City of Minnetonka, 176 F. Supp. 2d 926 (D. Minn. 2001)

Hog/Hobble Tie

Only use a hog-tie as a last resort and if you obtained the proper training, otherwise you could be liable for excessive force. Additionally, try not to use these restraints on suspects who have a diminished capacity such as:

- Severe intoxication

- Under the influence of a controlled substance

- Severe mental disability

REPORT WRITING

If you use a hog/hobble tie articulate the following:

1. Describe why this level of restraint was absolutely necessary;

2. If appropriate, articulate that the suspect did not appear to be severely intoxicated or highly impaired by a controlled substance;

3. Articulate that the suspect did not appear to have any medical conditions that would cause the suspect to have significant diminished capacity;

4. Describe how you visually monitored the suspect while he was in the restraints;

5. Describe that you did not leave the suspect on his stomach for longer than necessary;

6. Finally, articulate when you received training in this restraint method.

Note: Many people that require the hog-tie experience excited delirium, and therefore are highly susceptible to in-custody death. Get medical in route ASAP and have them evaluate the suspect.

Liability

Exclusionary Rule

The exclusionary rule states that evidence obtained as a result of an illegal search and/or seizure is inadmissible in a criminal trial. The purpose of the rule "is to deter future unlawful police conduct and thereby effectuate the guarantee of the Fourth Amendment against unreasonable searches and seizures."[1] It is also the purpose of the Fourth Amendment to "safeguard the privacy and security of individuals against arbitrary invasions by government officials."[2]

GUIDELINES

In order to successfully suppress evidence, the defendant must prove the following:

1. The defendant has standing to object. In other words, the defendant must prove the he has a reasonable expectation of privacy in the area searched or the thing seized;

2. Based solely on the evidence presented at the suppression hearing, the judge will determine whether the search or seizure was objectively unreasonable;

3. If the judge finds the search or seizure was unreasonable, he will decide whether the evidence should be suppressed;

- Suppression should only occur for deliberate, reckless or systemic error, not mere negligence;

- Suppression shouldn't occur if police can show that the evidence would have been inevitably discovered.

[1] United States v. Calandra, 414 U.S. 338 (U.S. 1974)
[2] Camara v. Municipal Court of San Francisco, 387 U.S. 523 (U.S. 1967)

Exceptions to the Exclusionary Rule

The exclusionary rule states that evidence obtained as a result of an illegal search and/or seizure is inadmissible in a criminal trial. This rule is meant to deter police misconduct.[1] But there are several exceptions.

GUIDELINES

Some exceptions to the exclusionary rule include:

1. The defendant has no standing to object;

2. Evidence can be used to impeach a defendant;

3. Good faith exception;

4. Foreign searches;

5. Inevitable discovery;

6. Deportation proceedings;

7. Grand juries;[2]

8. Sentencing proceedings; and

9. Civil tax proceedings.

---

[1] United States v. Leon, 468 U.S. 897 (U.S. 1984)
[2] United States v. Calandra, 414 U.S. 338 (U.S. 1974)

Exclusionary Rule and Attenuation

A court may admit evidence discovered after an illegal police search or seizure if the prosecution can show that there was no significant relationship between the unlawful conduct and the discovery of the evidence.[1] This is known as attenuation or an "intervening circumstance."

GUIDELINES

Factors used to determine if there was sufficient "attenuation" include:

1. The time proximity between the misconduct and discovery;

2. Whether there are other intervening circumstances; and

3. The purpose and flagrancy of the police misconduct.

CASE EXAMPLES

Arrest warrant attenuated illegal detention

"While Officer Fackrell's decision to initiate the stop was mistaken, his conduct thereafter was lawful...Moreover, there is no indication that this unlawful stop was part of any systemic or recurrent police misconduct. To the contrary, all the evidence suggests that the stop was an isolated instance of negligence that occurred in connection with a bona fide investigation of a suspected drug house...Applying these factors, we hold that the evidence discovered on Strieff's person was admissible because the unlawful stop was sufficiently attenuated by the pre-existing arrest warrant."[2]

---

[1] United States v. Ceccolini, 435 U.S. 268 (U.S. 1978)
[2] Utah v. Strieff, 136 S. Ct. 2056 (U.S. 2016)

Fruit of the Poisonous Tree

The exclusionary rule forbids the admission of illegally obtained evidence. The "fruit of the poisonous tree" doctrine says that any evidence found as a consequence of the first illegal search or seizure will also be suppressed.

This can get a little confusing but remember this, all illegally obtained evidence will usually be suppressed.

GUIDELINES

The fruit of the poisonous tree doctrine states that if police:

1. Conducted an illegal search and seizure; and

2. Additional evidence was ultimately obtained as a result of that illegal conduct, then that evidence will also be suppressed.

• Note, any evidence found after a search incident to an unlawful arrest would also be suppressed.

CASE EXAMPLES

Observations after unlawful entry cannot be used

Observations made after an unlawful, warrantless entry into a structure cannot be used to establish probable cause for later obtaining a search warrant.[1]

All evidence tainted after unlawful arrest

Where defendant was unlawfully arrested, evidence recovered from his person, incriminating statements, and the products of a search warrant that used all the above as part of its probable cause, were subject to being suppressed.[2]

---

[1] Murray v. United States, 487 U.S. 533 (U.S. 1988)
[2] United States v. Nora, 765 F.3d 1049 (9th Cir. Cal. 2014)

Standing

In order for a defendant to challenge the constitutionality of a search or seizure they must show that he had some "skin in the game." In other words, the actual search and seizure must have involved them in some material way.

It's helpful to the prosecution to ask ownership questions in the field. If someone denies ownership of a bag, purse, car, etc. that can help show they did not have standing to object to the search or seizure (even if they legally owned the item).

Guidelines

Standing means that a defendant must show that the illegal search or seizure invaded their own personal, reasonable, and legitimate expectation of privacy.[1]

Establishing "standing," however, can be tricky. Among the factors to be considered are:

1. Whether the defendant has a property or possessory interest in the thing seized or the place searched;

2. Whether he has the right to exclude others from the place or thing searched;

3. Whether he exhibited a subjective expectation that it would remain free from governmental invasion;

4. Whether he took normal precautions to maintain his privacy; and

5. Whether he was legitimately on the premises.[2]

---

[1] Minnesota v. Carter, 525 U.S. 83 (U.S. 1998)
[2] People v. Roybal, 19 Cal. 4th 481 (Cal. 1998)

Good Faith Exception

The Supreme Court outlined a "good faith exception" to the exclusionary rule.[1] For example, when police, in good faith, relied upon a warrant that was later found to be defective (e.g. lacked probable cause) any evidence found may be admitted during the trial.

The good faith exception also applies when police rely upon an existing law that is later found to be unconstitutional. It would serve no useful purpose to exclude evidence under these circumstances since there's no police misconduct.

GUIDELINES

There are three requirements:

1. The officer must have exhibited good faith, and been objectively reasonable in their beliefs;

2. Warrants must be issued by a "neutral and detached" judge; and

3. The warrant cannot be so lacking in P/C that a reasonable officer would know that the existence of P/C is entirely unreasonable.

CASE EXAMPLES

"Good faith" is based on objective reasonableness

In evaluating a "good faith" claim, the courts will look to whether a "reasonably well trained officer would have known that the search was illegal" in light of all the circumstances.[2] The officer's subjective belief is not a consideration. The inquiry looks to the objective facts only, which can include a particular officer's knowledge and experience but not the officer's subjective intent or belief.[3]

---

[1] United States v. Leon, 468 U.S. 897 (U.S. 1984)
[2] Id.
[3] Herring v. United States, 555 U.S. 135 (U.S. 2009)

Inevitable Discovery

The exclusionary rule forbids the admission of illegally obtained evidence. However, if the prosecution can show that the evidence would have been discovered irrespective of the illegal conduct, then the evidence will not be suppressed.

GUIDELINES

There are two requirements:

1. At the time of the misconduct there was an *independent* line of police investigation underway which developed facts which would have led to the discovery of the evidence; or

2. There was a standard procedure (e.g. vehicle inventory) in effect that would've inevitably turned up the same evidence.

CASE EXAMPLES

Police search party would have discovered tainted evidence

Police violated Miranda rights. Suspect eventually identified where child's body was buried. Evidence not suppressed because police had a search party in the area and would have likely discovered the remains anyway. Of course, suspect's admission where body was buried was suppressed.[1]

Evidence admissible if police show they would've gotten a warrant

"The doctrine may even apply where the subsequent search that inevitably would have uncovered the disputed evidence required a warrant and the police had probable cause to obtain this warrant ...*if* the government produces evidence that the police would have obtained the necessary warrant absent the illegal search."[2]

---

[1] Nix v. Williams, 467 U.S. 431 (U.S. 1984)
[2] United States v. Jones, 2016 U.S. Dist. LEXIS 71181 (W.D. Pa. June 1, 2016)

Duty to Protect

You have no legal or constitutional obligation to protect citizens from harm caused by third party, non-governmental actors.[1] This is true even if the injury was caused in your presence and you "could have done something." It's only at the point that you actually get involved, or somehow placed the third party in harm, that you can be held liable.

GUIDELINES

There must be a "special relationship" between you and the injured party before you can be held liable. Two common special relationships:

1. You arrested the suspect; or

2. You created or enhanced the danger to the victim.

CASE EXAMPLES

Police not liable for death of TPO victim

A suspect violated a TPO and fled the scene before police arrived. The suspect returned later and killed the applicant, even though police didn't look for the suspect.[2] Police had no special relationship with victim, and therefore were not liable. Note, liability would attach if police refused to arrest on-scene suspect.

Police liable for ejected bar patron that froze to death

Police were called about a drunk patron at a bar. Police ejected the patron into subzero temperatures and told him he was not allowed to drive home. The patron left the area wearing a t-shirt and jeans. He was found dead the next morning in an alley. Qualified immunity denied and family can move forward with their lawsuit.[3]

[1] Deshaney v. Winnebago County Dep't of Social Services, 489 U.S. 189 (U.S. 1989)
[2] Town of Castle Rock v. Gonzales, 545 U.S. 748 (U.S. 2005)
[3] Munger v. City of Glasgow Police Dep't, 227 F.3d 1082 (9th Cir. Mont. 2000)

§ 1983 Lawsuits

"1983" civil lawsuits are based on Federal code 42 U.S.C. § 1983. It's a common lawsuit and provides citizens with a remedy for violations of constitutionally-protected rights.

GUIDELINES

A 1983 violation consists of:

1. Violation of a constitutionally or federally protected right;

2. Violation must have occurred while acting "under the color of law."[1] In layman's term, if you're on-duty and doing your job, you're acting "under color of law;"

3. The plaintiff need not suffer actual harm. Nominal damages are available and court may award reasonable attorney's fees.

HYPOTHETICAL

Even if there's no real "damage" you can still be sued. For example, during a knock and talk you notice the garage door is open and without consent you enter and knock on the home's interior door. This is a clear violation of the Fourth Amendment (warrantless entry), yet a court may award $1 in nominal damages. But, his attorney would get "reasonable attorney's fees" and that could cost your agency tens of thousands of dollars.

CASE EXAMPLES

Probable cause is absolute defense

Probable cause is an absolute defense to any claim under § 1983 for wrongful arrest or false imprisonment.[2]

---

[1] Monroe v. Pape, 365 U.S. 167 (U.S. 1961)
[2] Bailey v. City of Chicago, 779 F.3d 689 (7th Cir. Ill. 2015)

§ 242 Criminal Actions

If you *intentionally* violate a person's constitutionally or federally protected rights, then you could be charged criminally under 18 U.S.C. § 242. Under a § 1983 suit, the plaintiff doesn't need to prove intent, here they do. That's why the DOJ reserves these actions for only the most egregious bad actors.

Remember Rodney King? Initially the LAPD cops were charged under state criminal statutes and were acquitted. That's when the DOJ came in and convicted the officers under § 242. Not good.

GUIDELINES

1. If an officer intentionally violates a person's constitutionally or federally protected rights, they can be charged criminally under state penal codes;

2. If the conduct is particularly egregious, the DOJ can charge the officer federally for violating § 242.

CASE EXAMPLES

Koon v. United States

"On August 4, 1992, a federal grand jury indicted the four officers under 18 U.S.C. § 242, charging them with violating King's constitutional rights under color of law. Powell, Briseno, and Wind were charged with *willful use of unreasonable force* in arresting King. Koon was charged with willfully permitting the other officers to use unreasonable force during the arrest. After a trial in United States District Court for the Central District of California, the jury convicted Koon and Powell but acquitted Wind and Briseno."[1]

---

[1] Koon v. United States, 518 U.S. 81 (U.S. 1996)

Failure to Intervene

You must intervene on behalf of a citizen whose constitutional rights are being violated by a government employee (everyone from cops to building inspectors). If not, you can be held vicariously liable and sued. This topic is a touchy one and no cop wants to be put in this situation. But remember, if you have to get involved it's not you that caused it, it's the other officer who failed to follow the rules. At the end of the day it's your career and family you need to think about.

GUIDELINES

You must intervene on behalf of a citizen whose constitutional rights are being violated by another government employee, especially another police officer.

CASE EXAMPLES

An officer must intervene, if they have an opportunity

A police officer "has a duty under § 1983 'to intervene to prevent a false arrest or the use of excessive force if the officer is informed of the facts that establish a constitutional violation and has the ability to prevent it.' Thus, in an excessive force case, a police officer who is present and does not intervene to stop other officers from infringing the constitutional rights of citizens is liable under § 1983 if the officer had reason to know "that excessive force was being used, . . . and the officer had a realistic opportunity to intervene to prevent the harm from occurring."[1]

---

[1] Smith v. Hunt, 2010 U.S. Dist. LEXIS 101526 (N.D. Ill. Sept. 27, 2010)

Supervisor Liability

Supervisors must supervise. If you fail to document misconduct and take corrective actions against a subordinate, you can be held liable for similar future misconduct even if you weren't directly involved.[1]

GUIDELINES

Supervisors can be held liable if:

- You had actual or constructive knowledge that a subordinate was engaged in conduct that posed a pervasive or unreasonable risk of constitutional violations;

- Your lack of response showed a deliberate indifference or tacit approval of the subordinate's conduct;

- There was a causal link between your inaction and the injury.

CASE EXAMPLES

Supervisor may be liable for failure to supervise

A supervisor may be held liable for the alleged unconstitutional acts of his subordinates if plaintiffs demonstrate an "affirmative link" that he actively participated or acquiesced in the constitutional violation. That "affirmative link" can be shown through the supervisor's personal participation, his exercise of control or direction, or his failure to supervise.[2]

Not liable for mere negligent supervision

"Supervisors who are merely negligent in failing to detect and prevent subordinates' misconduct are not liable."[3]

---

[1] Shaw v. Stroud, 13 F.3d 791 (4th Cir. N.C. 1994)
[2] Holland v. Harrington, 268 F.3d 1179 (10th Cir. Colo. 2001)
[3] Morfin v. City of E. Chicago, 349 F.3d 989 (7th Cir. Ind. 2003)

Unequal Enforcement of the Law

You will sometimes be criticized because you're not enforcing a law on everyone. For example, if you pull a subject over for speeding a common defense is that another person was speeding faster. This attack on your discretion is usually not a Fourth Amendment violation. In order to succeed, the suspect would have to prove you had no rational basis for choosing him over another suspect. In reality this is a very difficult thing to prove.

GUIDELINES

In order to win a civil suit a plaintiff must:

1. Show he was treated differently from others similarly situated, and

2. Prove there was no rational basis for the different treatment.

A "rational basis" could simply be that you can only enforce the law on one person at a time.

CASE EXAMPLE

Towing just one car is not unequal enforcement
Noble argues that the Mayor didn't like him and that's why he ordered his car towed. As it stands, "[a]ll it takes to defeat [Noble's] claim is a *conceivable* rational basis for the difference in treatment...If we can come up with a rational basis for the challenged action, that will be the end of the matter...a rational basis for the difference in treatment is that the Village cannot be expected to tow every inoperable vehicle at once."[1]

---

[1] Noble v. Vill. of Elliott, 605 Fed. Appx. 572 (7th Cir. Ill. 2015)

Shocks the Conscious

You can be liable if you had an intent and purpose to cause harm unrelated to the legitimate object of the arrest, or use of force.[1] This standard is much higher than gross negligence or deliberate indifference and is difficult for a plaintiff to meet.

GUIDELINES

The plaintiff must prove:

1. You had an intent and purpose to cause harm; and

2. It was unrelated to the legitimate object of arrest.

CASE EXAMPLES

Illegal home entry and stomach pumping shocked the conscious

"This is conduct that shocks the conscience: Illegally breaking into the privacy of a petitioner, the struggle to open his mouth and remove what was there, the forcible extraction of his stomach's contents -- this course of proceeding by agents of government to obtain evidence is bound to offend even hardened sensibilities."[2]

Digital rectum searches on prisoners shocked the conscious

"Under the facts as alleged by Vaughan, a reasonable prison official in 1984 would have understood that the [rectum] searches were conducted in a brutal fashion that was not justified by a need for force. The extent of possible injury was great, and at least one inmate suffered significant injury. The joking and insults directed at the inmates support an inference that the force was maliciously and sadistically applied."[3]

---

[1] County of Sacramento v. Lewis, 523 U.S. 833 (U.S. 1998)
[2] Rochin v. California, 342 U.S. 165 (U.S. 1952)
[3] Vaughan v. Ricketts, 859 F.2d 736 (9th Cir. Ariz. 1988)

Right to Disobey Unlawful Order

A citizen is under no legal obligation to obey an "unlawful order." For example, if you ordered a controversial group (i.e. Westboro Baptist Church) to stop protesting near city hall (legal conduct), they do not have to comply. Still, if you chose to make an "unlawful" arrest for disobeying a police officer, the citizen may not resist arrest. Their only remedy is to sue you.

GUIDELINES

A citizen has no obligation to comply with any unlawful order given by a police officer. If an officer chooses to make an arrest the officer can be sued (subject has no right to physically resist officer, even when enforcing an unlawful order).

A subject must comply with all orders issued by a court, lawful and unlawful.[1]

CASE EXAMPLES

Defendant did not obstruct police after they demanded entry without a warrant
> Police went to the defendant's house in search of a fugitive. They demanded entry and defendant asked if they had a warrant. 'When...the officer demands entry but presents no warrant, there is a presumption that the officer has no right to enter, because it is only in certain carefully defined circumstances that lack of a warrant is excused. An occupant can act on that presumption and refuse admission."[2] Obstruction charge overturned.

---

[1] Walker v. Birmingham, 87 S. Ct. 1824 (U.S. 1967)
[2] United States v. Prescott, 581 F.2d 1343 (9th Cir. Cal. 1978)

No Right to Resist Unlawful Arrest

Under common law citizens were allowed to physically resist an unlawful arrest.[1] But many jurisdictions are now deciding that a citizen may not resist any arrest, lawful or unlawful.

The courts have stated that allowing citizens the right to resist an unlawful arrest is a recipe for disaster because citizens can get seriously hurt (or killed) since modern law enforcement has the tools and training to overcome most resistance. The better solution is to let the judge decide if the arrest was an unlawful arrest and allow the citizen to sue if necessary.

GUIDELINES

1. A subject may not physically resist an unlawful arrest. The initial "unlawful" charge will be dismissed, but the citizen can be lawfully charged with assault and battery on an officer;

2. A person can sue for being unlawfully arrested.

CASE EXAMPLES

Illegal arrest didn't justify resisting officer

Officers located two males matching an anonymous caller's description of persons involved in a recent disturbance. After repeatedly ignoring the officers' commands to sit on the ground, suspect threatened officers, resisted a control hold, and punched one of them. The court found that any Fourth Amendment violation could not result in the suppression of evidence of the assault on the officer and resisting arrest.[2]

---

[1] Elk v. United States, 177 U.S. 529 (U.S. 1900)
[2] In re Richard G., 173 Cal. App. 4th 1252 (Cal. App. 2d Dist. 2009)

Summary Judgment

If police get sued, the first thing the government attorney will often try to do is get the case dismissed under summary judgment. The strategy here is simple; the government attorney will argue that even if the facts laid out by the plaintiff are materially correct, there's no constitutional violation.

GUIDELINES

1. In considering the summary judgment, the court will consider the facts most favorable to the non-moving party (plaintiff);

2. Determine if there are any genuine issues of material fact;

3. If there are no genuine issues of material facts, and the government attorney successfully argued why there was no constitutional violation, the case will be dismissed.

CASE EXAMPLES

If there are material dispute of facts, summary judgment is not appropriate

In a civil suit for the use of excessive, deadly force, where the officer/defendant moves for summary judgment, the trial court must look at the evidence in the light most favorable to the plaintiff with respect to the central facts of the case. In this case, where the officer shot the plaintiff in the chest, the Fifth Circuit failed to acknowledge and credit plaintiff's evidence with regard to the lighting, his mother's demeanor, whether he shouted words that were an overt threat, and his positioning during the shoot." Summary judgment was not appropriate in this case.[1]

---

[1] Tolan v. Cotton, 134 S. Ct. 1861 (U.S. 2014)

Qualified Immunity

Police officers work in dynamic and unpredictable environments. Therefore, officers encounter situations where they are tasked to solve unique problems despite no applicable training or case law to guide them. Qualified immunity protects officers whenever they venture into constitutionally unchartered territories.

GUIDELINES

1. Officers would receive qualified immunity when their particular conduct is not clearly established at the time the officer undertook the conduct in question;

2. No qualified immunity for conduct that obviously violates rights.

CASE EXAMPLES

Officer that attempted knock and talk on side door, versus front door, entitled to qualified immunity

It is an open, undecided issue, with authority going both ways, as to whether it is lawful for an officer to conduct a "knock and talk" at other than the front door. A trooper was sued by homeowners because he knocked on a side door, instead of the front door. The Supreme Court determined that the officer was entitled to qualified immunity in that the issue is the subject of conflicting authority.[1]

No qualified immunity for prison guard who obviously violated rights

Guard who handcuffed shirtless prisoner to hitching post as punishment not eligible for qualified immunity since it obviously violated the Fourth Amendment.[2]

---

[1] Carroll v. Carman, 135 S. Ct. 348 (U.S. 2014)
[2] Hope v. Pelzer, 536 U.S. 730 (U.S. 2002)

Media Entry into Homes

Generally, you cannot take non-essential personnel into an area protected by the Fourth Amendment, particularly a home.

GUIDELINES

You cannot bring non-essential personnel into protected areas unless you have consent, this includes members of the media and may include citizen ride-alongs.

CASE EXAMPLES

Bringing media into the home is a violation

"It is a violation of [Fourth Amendment] for police to bring members of the media or other third parties into a home" while police perform their duties.[1]

Evidence will not be excluded if media violate this rule

A Guam Police Department search warrant resulted in one of the largest busts of stolen items in Guam's history. The "woefully inadequate" management of the search of the residence attracted members of the media and victims who came to claim their property while the two-day execution of the warrant was ongoing. Although the conduct of the search was highly questionable, given the participation of the public and the media, the district court did not err by deciding not to exclude the stolen items, drugs, and other paraphernalia found in the compound.[2]

---

[1] Wilson v. Layne, 526 U.S. 603 (U.S. 1999)
[2] United States v. Duenas, 691 F.3d 1070 (9th Cir. Guam 2012)

Sharing Crime Scene Photos on Social Media

You can be held civilly liable for taking pictures of crime scenes and sharing them with friends or other outsiders, when not in the course of official business. Additionally, the defense can subpoena your personal cell phone for inspection.

Do not take pictures of any crime scene with your phone, it's unprofessional and can get you fired and sued.

GUIDELINES

Elements of Invasion of Privacy:

1. Public disclosure;

2. Of a private fact;

3. Which would be offensive and objectionable to a reasonable person; and

4. Which is not protected by the First Amendment.

CASE EXAMPLES

CHP officer liable for sharing accident scene photos with friends

Once photographic evidence is collected, it is not the role of the CHP... to distribute that evidence to friends and family members. [And] it is not the role of the CHP to put the parents and siblings of the decedent at risk of harm of seeing the grotesque death images of their deceased loved one made the subject of Internet spectacle.[1]

---

[1] Catsouras v. Department of California Highway Patrol, 181 Cal. App. 4th 856 (Cal. App. 4th Dist. 2010)

About the Author

Anthony Bandiero is a retired law enforcement officer with experience as both a municipal police officer and sergeant with a state police agency. Anthony has studied constitutional law for over fifteen years and has trained numerous police officers in advanced search and seizure.

Anthony has an associate's degree from the College of Southern Nevada, both a bachelor's and master's degree from Harvard University in liberal arts and government, respectively. Anthony is also a graduate of Northwestern University's School of Police Staff and Command and a Certified Public Manager (CPM). He is currently pursuing his Juris Doctor at Gonzaga University's School of Law.

Blue to Gold Law Enforcement Training is a company dedicated to law enforcement search and seizure training. For more information or to contact Anthony visit:

BlueToGold.com or email info@BlueToGold.com

82225951R00154

Made in the USA
Lexington, KY
27 February 2018